Cowher Power

Pittsburgh Post-Gazette

Pittsburgh Post-Gazette

John Robinson Block, Publisher and Editor in Chief
David M. Shribman, Executive Editor and Vice President
Susan L. Smith, Managing Editor
Mary C. Leonard, Deputy Managing Editor
Jerry Micco, Assistant Managing Editor/Sports

Cowher Power edited by

Donna Eyring, Sports Editor

Statistics research

Ken Mrazik, Sports News Assistant

Photo Editor

Larry Roberts

Photographers

Peter Diana	Steve Mellon	Andy Starnes	Bill Wade
Matt Freed	John Beale	John Heller	Franka Bruns
Lake Fong	Annie O'Neill	Darrell Sapp	Gabor Degra
Robin Rombach	Tony Tye	Bob Donaldson	Douglass Oster

Published by Triumph Books, Chicago.

Content packaged by Mojo Media, Inc.

Joe Funk, Editor
Mike Stokes, Copy Editor
Jason Hinman, Creative Director

This book is available in quantity at special discounts for your group or organization.
For further information, contact:

Triumph Books
542 South Dearborn Street, Suite 750
Chicago, Illinois, 60605
(312) 939-3330   Fax: (312) 663-3557

Printed in the United States of America

Lake Fong

Contents

Foreword

By Ron Cook

As a sports-loving high-school senior, Bill Cowher didn't dream of coaching his hometown Pittsburgh Steelers and winning a Super Bowl and handing that beautiful Vince Lombardi Trophy to a beaming member of the Rooney family. Like his buddies at Carlynton High and his neighborhood pals in Crafton, a suburb west of Pittsburgh, he watched with great joy as Chuck Noll gave that marvelous piece of hardware to The Chief, Art Rooney Sr., after the Steelers won the first of their four Super Bowls in the 1970s on a wondrous day in New Orleans in January 1975. But Cowher didn't want to be like the great Noll, a legendary coach. He wanted to be Terry Bradshaw or Joe Greene or maybe Jack Lambert. He wanted to play the game, play it at its highest level, play it in the National Football League. A few months later, he would leave for North Carolina State on a football scholarship. He never did become another Bradshaw, Greene or Lambert, but he did get to live his dream and play five seasons in the NFL. He would have played a lot longer, too, if his talent had been more plentiful and his knee hadn't given out.

That was OK, though. Football was a wonderful life and Cowher's guardian angel, Marty Schottenheimer, his old coach with the Cleveland Browns, offered him a chance to get into coaching. For four seasons he worked with Schottenheimer in Cleveland, then three more with him in Kansas City as the Chiefs' defensive coordinator, all the while building a reputation as one of the game's hot-shot young coaching prospects. Isn't it funny how life works sometimes? The Steelers' job came open after the 1991 season when Noll retired. Schottenheimer gave Cowher a heck of a recommendation. The next thing anyone knew, the Crafton kid, still only 34, was coming home to take the most prestigious job in town, no disrespect to all of those wonderful docs at the world-renowned Pittsburgh hospitals.

It's fair to say that it was then that Cowher started having that dream about the Super Bowl trophy. Rooney Sr. was gone, but his son, Dan, was the same type of good man, just about the best boss anyone could want. Blue-collar. Hard-working. Wise. Loyal ... Loyal beyond belief, actually. Together, Rooney and Cowher started a relationship that became unlike any other at the time in the NFL. They shared so many good moments. Eight division championships in Cowher's first 13 seasons. Nine trips to the playoffs. Five AFC championship games. A trip to Super Bowl XXX to play the Dallas Cowboys. "Cowher Power" became a popular catch phrase in Pittsburgh. But, of course, Rooney and Cowher also shared some hard times. Life isn't always perfect, you know. From 1998-2000, the Steelers went 7-9, 6-10 and 9-7 and missed the playoffs all three seasons. Cowher

Cowher Power

wasn't much of a hometown hero then. He was tortured by the local media and fans, especially on that relatively new wonder of the world, the Internet, where nameless, faceless people can offer the rudest, cruelest opinions in total anonymity. Coaching the Steelers might be a prestigious job, but the man doing it is constantly scrutinized. And the scrutiny can be brutal.

It was enough to test even the strongest of relationships, but Rooney never wavered. He stuck with Cowher when probably no other NFL owner would have. "He always conducted himself the way I thought he should," Rooney said years later. "He's a good coach and good person." Said Cowher: "I'll always appreciate that patience." That's why, after the Steelers beat the Denver Broncos in the AFC championship after the 2005 season, Cowher, now a grizzled coach nearing the end of his 14th season, immediately looked ahead to the possibility of winning Super Bowl XL and finally being able to give Rooney that trophy. "Nothing would make me more satisfied," he said, his big jaw jutting like never before. "Nothing drives me more."

That day in Denver had special meaning for Cowher for personal reasons. For too long, he had been reminded that he couldn't win the big games. His regular-season success was extraordinary, Hall of Fame-like, an astonishing average of just more than 10 wins a year. But, before Denver, he was 1-4 in AFC title games, the losses all at home. He also was a loser in Super Bowl XXX. Even in 2004, when the Steelers ran off to a 15-1 regular-season record, Cowher couldn't enjoy it. "I know I'm way beyond anything less than a championship now," he said. "It's no longer about winning divisions or getting to the Super Bowl. It's about winning a championship. That's how I'll be judged."

Wouldn't you know the Steelers were then beaten at home in the AFC championship game by the New England Patriots?

For a long time it didn't look as if Cowher would get another chance in 2005. Because quarterback Ben Roethlisberger missed four games with a knee injury, the Steelers were 7-5 after losing at home to the Cincinnati Bengals, their third consecutive loss. The Super Bowl seemed out of the question. Even the playoffs looked like a reach. But Cowher, doing perhaps his best coaching job, kept his team together. He instructed his players to forget about the past and the future, to concentrate only on the next week's opponent, the Chicago Bears. After they beat the Bears, he said the same thing about the Minnesota Vikings and then the Cleveland Browns and, finally, the Detroit Lions. The Steelers won every game. They might have sneaked into the playoffs as the AFC's No. 6 team, but they were rolling, as confident a bunch as Cowher has had in the post-season. They beat the Bengals to give him his first road playoff victory. They shocked the Indianapolis Colts in Indianapolis. And they stunned the Broncos.

Now, all that was left was Super Bowl XL.

Steelers fans will long remember the many unforgettable moments from their team's 21-10 win against the Seattle Seahawks at Detroit's Ford Field. Jerome Bettis, playing his final NFL game in his hometown, being sent out alone by his teammates during the pregame introductions to bask in the adulation one last time. Roethlisberger diving for the end zone. Willie Parker going 75 yards off right tackle. Ike Taylor picking off a Matt Hasselbeck pass. Antwaan Randle El throwing a touchdown pass to Hines Ward. Ward smiling that electric smile as he skipped into the end zone.

Cowher will remember all of those same moments and more. But the one he'll remember most is lifting that gorgeous Lombardi Trophy and presenting it to Rooney, much the way Noll had done for The Chief a lifetime earlier. Clearly, it was the realization of his greatest NFL dream. ✦

The Jewel in the Crown

By Ed Bouchette

After 14 years as a head coach, Bill Cowher has become an overnight sensation. It's as if the first dirty dozen or so were a work in progress that was hailed in whole when he raised the Lombardi Trophy in Detroit.

Life may not be dramatically different for Cowher, but the perception of him certainly is. It's as if all those regular-season wins were validated by one victory in the Super Bowl.

"Now it happens and you continue to get congratulations. I guess that's what keeps your mind on it," Cowher said of the crowning achievement to his NFL career. "There's a lot more attention. I've had to adjust to that. It's been great, though. It's a lot better than . . . . 'Oh, you guys still had a heck of a year.' "

He really has had a good run over 14 years, making the playoffs 10 times, coaching in six AFC championship games and two Super Bowls, but the victory in Super Bowl XL put him on another level. No more can anyone claim he can't win the big one, something that dogged him as he dragged an 8-9 post-season record into the 2005 playoffs.

"I guess the last few years I probably have refused to think about winning," Cowher said. "I probably was more afraid of losing because I've been so close."

In private moments, Cowher has talked about the frustration of losing so many close games in AFC championships, such as those to San Diego and Denver in the 1990s. He also recalled 2001 when the Steelers easily outgained the New England Patriots but lost by 7 points because of a punt and a blocked field goal attempt that were each returned for touchdowns.

He spoke openly in the two weeks before the Feb. 5 Super Bowl about the pain of losing Super Bowl XXX to Dallas.

That pain is now gone.

"Let's be honest," Cowher said. "Every year you sit back and reflect, and you think, 'How many times are you going to be asked the question, 'If you don't win the Super Bowl, will your career have been successful?' I've been very consistent in saying no, there'd be a void that would always be there."

He no longer gets those questions. Now there are pats on the back, and most are genuine.

"A lot of coaches feel good for him," said his mentor, San Diego coach Marty Schottenheimer, who for all his regular-season greatness is still searching to make his first Super Bowl visit. "He and I were talking the other day, and I said it's harder now to win a championship in the NFL. It's hard — you have to get the stars aligned correctly."

Steelers President Art Rooney, who stuck with Cowher during a stretch of three years in which the team went 7-9, 6-10 and 9-7 and missed the playoffs, never wavered in his support.

"He's done a great job," Rooney said. "I was really

Cowher Power

Bill Cowher waves to Steeler fans after beating the Browns in Cleveland.

happy he got that last feather in his cap. He deserves to go down as one of the great coaches we've had and that the game has had. The level of consistency that our team has performed at over his tenure has been pretty remarkable, given free agency and everything else we have in this day and age.

"It was great for him to win it. I think it would be great for him to repeat. I think that would put him at another sort of level in the hierarchy of all-time coaches. He's that kind of coach who will distinguish himself."

Cowher, who turned 49 years old in the spring of 2006, has an opportunity to post numbers among the NFL's greatest coaches. He already ranks 14th all-time in regular-season victories with a record of 141-82-1. But it's one year at a time for Cowher, who would love to add another Super Bowl victory, or more.

"When you have opportunities that we have in front of us to do that, you have to ride it," Cowher said. "We have a lot of people back. It's not going to be easy, it's a big challenge, but boy, to me it's very invigorating. I think we're all kind of champing at the bit to get back."

"In this business, it's really important that you stay focused on the next year," Cowher said. "I've been in that mindset the last few years. It allows you to maybe coach with a sense of urgency that you have to have in this business.

"I think the longer I stayed in it the more I realized every year is a very special year. That's how we approached last year and I can't see approaching this any different than we did last year."

It would surprise no one if Cowher coached the Steelers another 10 years, nor if he quit after the next one or two, moved to Raleigh, N.C., where he

Bill Cowher and Larry Foote look at the referees in disbelief after a ruling.

recently bought a house, and contemplated his future and possible return with another team. Many others have done it before him, including Schottenheimer and Dick Vermeil, the only two who coached him as a player in the NFL, along with Bill Parcells, Jimmy Johnson and even the great Vince Lombardi.

For now, though, his Steelers are stocked with enough talent to make a repeat run, and the prospect of winning two consecutive Super Bowls drives him.

"Whether we won it or lost it, to me it's about starting back over again and the challenges that go with that," Cowher said. "You can have a lot to refer to — we all understood the excitement about what we were able to experience and I think that can be a motivating factor. As long as we recognize it's not going to pick right back up where we left off, there's lot of hard work, sacrifice and a big commitment."

The commitment is there for 2006, perhaps even for 2007. Beyond that is anyone's guess. ✦

Cowher Power

Bill Cowher argues a call with line judge Jerome Boger in Indianapolis.

Peter Diana

1992

Cowher Aiming High, But Wide

Super Bowl talk an unrealistic dream for team lacking championship talent

Legend has it that when Chuck Noll addressed his first Steelers team in the summer of 1969, he informed the assembled players that few of them had what it took to play in the National Football League. Upbeat Bill Cowher, who succeeded Noll, has made no such pronouncement to his first Steelers team.

But could he?

Coaches no longer talk to athletes the way Noll did 23 years ago. But if Cowher weren't such an optimist and the modern players weren't so sensitive, maybe this team would deserve a similar message.

If there were a dispersal draft of the Steelers, none of the other 27 NFL teams would be smacking their lips. There are several reasons the Steelers have just about the lowest payroll in the NFL, and talent is one of them.

Still Cowher talks Super Bowl. He should be talking winning season. Even in the mildly pathetic Central Division of the American Football Conference, the Steelers will have difficulty winning more games than they lose. If they succeed, team president Dan Rooney has made his second consecutive brilliant coaching hire.

Cowher brought in Ron Erhardt to install his power offense that was so successful, for a time, with the New York Giants. But where's the power? Where's the big, bruising back who will grind out the yardage this run-oriented offense must generate?

Tim Worley best fit that role, but he has been suspended for the season. Every back in the NFL should have the work ethic of Merril Hoge, but he's not the answer for 16 weeks. Barry Foster might be, but he is so pouty and sullen about what he perceives as an economic slight by the Steelers that his effectiveness is in question.

And running back doesn't figure to be one of the major weaknesses.

Remember when people said wide receiver was the easiest position to fill in the NFL, that the land was overrun with fast guys with incredible athletic talent?

Why can't the Steelers find them?

Louis Lipps once was the answer, but not anymore. Dwight Stone never was. And maybe there was a logical reason Noll didn't take a closer look at Jeff Graham and Ernie Mills, the second and third-round draft choices last year.

Noll was stubborn, but nobody's fool. Already, Charles Davenport, this season's No. 4, is impressing more people than Graham or Mills.

The offensive line hardly appears to be a strength, even with the addition of Leon Searcy, the No. 1 draft choice from Miami. The fact Searcy is given a chance to move into the starting lineup says a lot about the inadequacy of the line.

What this mediocre band of running backs, wide receivers and offensive linemen needs to bring

Cowher Power

Bill Cowher at minicamp, May 1, 1992

Tony Tye

Andy Starnes

them together and take them to a title is a quarterback of wondrous talent and a winning background. But the Steelers' quarterbacks have neither attribute and, instead, desperately require precisely the supporting cast the Steelers lack.

Neither four-year starter Bubby Brister nor third-year man Neil O'Donnell has done anything to indicate he can take the Steelers to Cowher's goals.

Tight ends Eric Green and Adrian Cooper will significantly help this otherwise beleaguered offense.

The defense should be better than the offense, but not good enough to win games by itself.

So why is Cowher talking Super Bowl?

"I talk high goals because I don't believe you can achieve something you don't set. If you go in with the idea of just making the playoffs or having a winning record, when you attain that, then you feel a sense of accomplishment, and the only team in the National Football League that should feel a sense of accomplishment is the team that wins the Super Bowl."

Cowher knows it won't be easy. He knows it will take something special, maybe something not really possible.

"We need to have some of our veterans play the best football of their careers. We have to have some young people come in and contribute."

Sounds like Cowher is asking a lot. ✦

Cowher Power

Carlynton High School

Cowher was a Crafton, Pa. native and a standout linebacker for Carlynton High School in 1975.

1992 Game Of The Year:
A Chief Mission

Cowher calls trip to Kansas City 'just our seventh game'

At least Marty Schottenheimer won't have to worry about getting run over on the sideline.

Steelers Coach Bill Cowher returns to Kansas City Sunday, Oct. 25, returns to where his coaching career got its biggest boost, returns to face the man who is without question his mentor and professional role model.

Cowher spent three seasons with the Chiefs as defensive coordinator, a position he held until the Steelers hired him Jan. 21 to replace Chuck Noll, but he doesn't want to make too much of his return to Arrowhead Stadium even though the television networks do.

The game will be televised at 8:30 p.m. on WPXI and TNT.

"I don't want to take away and magnify the game because I still believe it's not a critical game," Cowher said. "It just happens to be our seventh game of the season. But there's no question I had a child born in Kansas City and obviously the coaching staff there is the staff I coached with for seven years, so it will be special. But nothing out of the ordinary."

Cowher said two weeks ago his return to Cleveland — where he spent three seasons as a player, four as an assistant coach — was not a big deal because he had already returned there as an assistant with the Chiefs.

But this is different. Cowher not only returns to face the Chiefs for the first time since he left, he returns as a young head coach who already has gained national recognition for instilling fervor in a dormant franchise.

Cowher is the second of the nine first-year head coaches in the National Football League this season to return to face the team he formerly coached. Indianapolis Colts Coach Ted Marchibroda played in Buffalo on Sept. 20.

"It's hard for me to put in perspective," Cowher said. "I just don't want to take away the focus of the game where it should be placed and that's on the players. But I think everyone is aware of the scenario that exists."

Many of the schedules and practice regimens the Steelers use were inherited from Schottenheimer, who is the only coach for whom Cowher has worked. Cowher began coaching at 28 — a knee injury with the Philadelphia Eagles ended his playing career — when Schottenheimer hired him to coach the Browns' special teams.

It was there that Schottenheimer learned not to get in the way of Cowher's work.

Literally.

Cowher was so intense he would run alongside his coverage teams on the sideline. Schottenheimer said he approved of the method ... until Cowher flattened him on the sideline.

Though he remains intense, Cowher has toned down the sideline histrionics with his new team, which will be playing its fifth road game of the season. That the game is against his former teacher underscores the fact it is the first of four consecutive meetings against 1991 playoff teams.

After the Chiefs, the Steelers play the Houston Oilers at home Nov. 1, at Buffalo on Nov. 8, and the Detroit Lions at home Nov. 15.

"I have a lot of respect for Marty Schottenheimer, but we're both in situations where we're preparing our football teams for the other," Cowher said. "When Sunday comes it's a question of being able to execute the plans we have implemented. I think the one thing that's going to be obvious is there's going to be an understating of the two teams, maybe a little more insight into the personnel that you may not have with a lot with other teams." ✦

1992 Analysis:
The Pluses, Minuses Of Steelers' Successful Year

Surprisingly, the Steelers have a chance to post their best record and win their first American Football Conference title since 1979, despite undergoing a major transformation.

They began the 1992 season with a new coach, all but one new assistant coaches, a new quarterback, a new featured running back, a new top receiver, a new outside linebacker and a new safety.

What's more, they began the season without three of their past five No. 1 draft choices, then played most of the season without their top tight end. And yet they have a chance to record the best record in the AFC and gain home-field advantage for the playoffs.

Here is a third-quarter report card on the 1992 Steelers:

Quarterback

Neil O'Donnell has slumped statistically in recent weeks, failing to pass for more than 200 yards in four of the past five games. But he has stayed away from the mistakes that plagued his predecessor, Bubby Brister, throwing only six interceptions in the first 11 games for the lowest interception ratio (2.0) in the AFC. When called on to replace O'Donnell against the Indianapolis Colts, Brister did what he had to do — win. **Grade: B+.**

Running backs

Barry Foster has set club records for most yards and most 100-yard games in a season, records previously held by Franco Harris, and has a chance to become the first Steelers player since Bill Dudley in 1946 to lead the NFL in rushing. He still has a shot at the NFL record for most 100-yard games in a season (12), set by Eric Dickerson in 1984 when he was with the Los Angeles Rams. He is responsible for 73 percent of the running plays, 42.4 percent of the total offense. **Grade: A+.**

Wide receivers

Jeff Graham was an early sensation replacing Louis Lipps, catching 34 passes for 536 yards in the first six games, then was slowed by rib and ankle injuries. Dwight Stone has dropped fewer passes this season and has been effective running reverses. When Graham was out, Ernie Mills showed an ability to catch tough passes over the middle. **Grade: B.**

Tight ends

A tough position to read, mainly because of early injuries to Eric Green and rookie Russ Campbell, then Green's six-game suspension for violating the league's drug policy. The Steelers have not been able to use the three-tight end offense that offensive coordinator Ron Erhardt loves. Adrian Cooper always has been a devastating blocker, but he only had two receptions in a recent six-game stretch. **Grade: C.**

Offensive line

Probably the biggest surprise of the season. Duval Love, a Plan B acquisition, has solidified the left guard position, long a trouble spot. Right guard Carlton Haselrig has become an accomplished run blocker in only his second season as a starter. And, after a three-game stint in which he shared time with Justin Strzelczyk, left tackle John Jackson allowed one sack — to Buffalo's Pro Bowl end Bruce Smith. **Grade: A.**

Defensive line

Another position hard to gauge because the Steelers used their dime defense (only two linemen) in six of the first 11 games. Gerald Williams was playing very well until he missed six games with a knee injury. Donald Evans continues to be the most no matter the defense. But Kenny Davidson and Aaron Jones still have to learn to pressure the passer from the outside. Until the Jerrol Williams have been asked to line up as defensive ends in the dime defense and that usually limits their effectiveness because they are going against offensive linemen 50 to 60 pounds heavier. But Lloyd is having another Pro Bowl-type season, leading the team in sacks, forced fumbles and fumble recoveries. Despite his contract squabbles, Hardy Nickerson leads the team in tackles. David Little is the odd-man out in the dime defense, but he had three sacks against the Bengals. **Grade: B.**

Secondary

Rod Woodson has redefined the cornerback position with his big-play ability and should be considered for the NFL's Defensive Player of the Year award, despite his troubles in Green Bay. Cornerback D.J. Johnson would get Pro Bowl consideration if hault of rookie safety Darren Perry, who has made surprisingly few mistakes. **Grade: A-.**

Special teams

Got started on the right foot when the fake-punt pass to Warren Williams propelled the Steelers to their season-opening victory in Houston. The Steelers have yielded the NFL's second highest kick return average, but Woodson has returned one punt fd by a disputed illegal block against Solomon Wilcots. The long-snapping duties that plagued the Steelers last year have seemingly been solved by rookie Kendall Gammon. And, after a slow start, punter Mark Royals averaged 45 yards on 24 punts in a five-gameh-down call in the first quarter against the Oilers in the season opener, then followed with a fake punt and two reverses. **Grade: A.**

Cowher Power

REGULAR SEASON (11-5)

Date	Visitor		Home	
9/6/92	Steelers	29	Oilers	24
9/13/92	Jets	10	Steelers	27
9/20/92	Steelers	23	Chargers	6
9/27/92	Steelers	3	Packers	17
10/11/92	Steelers	9	Browns	17
10/19/92	Bengals	0	Steelers	20
10/25/92	Steelers	27	Chiefs	3
11/1/92	Oilers	20	Steelers	21

Date	Visitor		Home	
11/8/92	Steelers	20	Bills	28
11/15/92	Lions	14	Steelers	17
11/22/92	Colts	14	Steelers	30
11/29/92	Steelers	21	Bengals	9
12/6/92	Seahawks	14	Steelers	20
12/13/92	Steelers	6	Bears	30
12/20/92	Vikings	6	Steelers	3
12/27/92	Browns	13	Steelers	23

PLAYOFFS

Date	Visitor		Home	
1/9/93	Bills	24	Steelers	3

INDIVIDUAL STATS

PASSING

Name	CMP	ATT	PCT	YDs	YPC	TDs	INTs	Sacks	Rating
O'Donnell	185	313	59.1	2283	12.3	13	9	27	75.6
Brister	63	116	54	719	11.4	2	5	13	56.7
Royals	1	1	100	42	42	0	0	0	95.8
Foster	0	1	0	0	0	0	0	0	39.6

RUSHING

Name	ATT	YDS	AVG	TDs
Foster	390	1690	4	11
Thompson	35	157	5	1
Hoge	41	150	4	0
Stone	12	118	10	0
Mills	1	20	20	0
Brister	10	16	2	0
O'Donnell	27	5	0	1
Williams	2	0	0	0

RECEIVING

Name	REC	YDS	AVG	TDs
Graham	49	711	15	1
Stone	34	501	15	3
Mills	30	383	13	3
Foster	36	344	10	0
Thompson	22	278	13	0
Hoge	28	231	8	1
Cooper	16	197	12	3
Green	14	152	11	2
Davenport	9	136	15	0
Williams	1	44	44	0
Didio	3	39	13	0
Jorden	6	28	4.7	2
Thigpen	1	2	2	0

KICKING

Name	XP	XPA	FG	FGA	Points
Anderson	29	31	28	36	113

PUNTING

Name	att	avg	Inside 20
Royals	73	43	22

INTERCEPTIONS

Name	INT
Perry	6
Johnson	5
Woodson	4
Griffin	3
Little	2
Williams	1
Lloyd	1

SACKS

Name	Sacks
Lloyd	7
Williams	5
Little	3
Evans	3
Williams	3
Lake	2
Nickerson	2
Howe	2
Davidson	2
Jones	2

1993

Second-and-goal

For an encore, Cowher expects Steelers to learn

By Gerry Dulac, Post-Gazette Sports Writer

Bill Cowher walks into his second season as Steelers coach with no quarterback debate, no uncertainty about his offense, no questions about the competency and chemistry of his coaching staff and no spectre of the former coach looming over his head like a guillotine with a frayed rope.

Cowher has assumed such control of this team that in less than one year he already is under a different form of pressure that many did not expect him to endure when he replaced Chuck Noll: That as defending Central Division champion, the team that tied for the best record (11-5) in the American Football Conference playoffs.

"That was a great experience for us," Cowher said. "We hadn't been in that position before. There's something to be said for being in playoffs. You experience all the hoopla that leads up to it and the game itself. There's something to be said for teams who have been there. They understand there's a maturity that takes place that allows you to take your game up to another level."

And that is what Cowher wants to do as the Steelers prepare to open their season next Sunday against the San Francisco 49ers at Three Rivers Stadium, the first step in what Cowher hopes will be a learning experience after last season's playoff loss to the Buffalo Bills.

Last year the theme was win the division, get home-field advantage and rely historically on the notion that teams with the most home playoff games have the best chance of making it to the Super Bowl.

The battle cry remains much the same this year with a different twist: The past three Super Bowl winners — New York Giants, Washington Redskins and Dallas Cowboys — had lost the previous year in the playoffs. And the Steelers want to benefit from their first-round elimination in 1992.

"I think what you see is a team that has more confidence than a year ago, and it should," Cowher said. "You can talk about it all you want, but until you experience it and go out and have success, only then do you have true confidence. It might have been something you're trying to create as opposed to something that may be there."

Cowher may have attempted to create such inner confidence with his fiery, rah-rah approach that carried the Steelers through the early part of last year. But by the time the Steelers reached Kansas City on Oct. 25, their psyches had transcended the world of creative cockiness and settled into a more detemined, less rehearsed attitude conviction.

The Steelers played their most complete game of the season against the Chiefs that Monday night, winning convincingly, 27-3, in Arrowhead Stadium,

Cowher Power

John Heller

Greg Lloyd stops the Saints' Dalton Hilliard and gets a hug from Chad Brown during a 37-14 Steelers victory.

then went on to win six of their final nine games. Included in that was three consecutive wins against division opponents that gave the Steelers a combined 5-1 record against the Oilers, Browns and Bengals.

Now Cowher heads into the season with a Pro Bowl running back who led the AFC in rushing (Barry Foster), a quarterback who finished as the third-rated passer in the AFC and ended up in the Pro Bowl (Neil O'Donnell), an offensive line that features maybe the best center in the NFL (Dermontti Dawson) and a Pro Bowl guard who is still learning the game (Carlton Haselrig), and a secondary featuring Pro Bowler Rod Woodson that is probably unmatched around the league.

"The No. 1 thing we wanted to establish last year was a mentality of running the football, of being a tough football team," Cowher said. "That obvi-

Greg Lloyd, Kenny Davidson and Kevin Greene stop Bengals running back Harold Greene at the line of scrimmage.

ously required us to find out about the offensive line, find out about the running backs, see if we had people who could accept that responsibility. I think we did that. I think our football team has taken on that identity."

Nobody accepted the responsibility more determinedly than Foster, a third-year running back who carried a club-record 390 times — an average of 24 per game — and rushed for a a club-record 1,690 yards, second only to Dallas' Emmitt Smith in the NFL.

Because of that, Foster wants a contract extension that would, among other things, place him among

Cowher Power

Neil O'Donnell hugs receiver Dwight Stone after Stone scored a fourth-quarter touchdown on an end-around.

Chargers quarterback John Friesz is knocked out of the game by Kevin Greene.

the top-paid running backs in the league. Foster might disappoint the Steelers with his mouth, but his performance on the field is another matter. Even with the stellar pre-season showing of former No. 1 pick Tim Worley, who is returning from a one-year drug suspension, Foster remains the focal point of the offense.

"A year ago we talked with Barry on a weekly basis to make sure he could handle it," Cowher said of Foster's workload. "While the carries added up, there were never really any signs of Barry being overworked."

In all likelihood, Foster will not even approach the number of carries he had last season, especially if the Steelers carry through on their promise to throw more and throw deeper in 1993. Also, the addition of Worley will give Cowher a chance to rest Foster and spare his body a little more frequently.

Cowher said Worley was given a lot of work in

the preseason because the Steelers want to see if he has the durability, something he has not always displayed in the past, to stand up to the punishment.

"I think Timmy still has some things to prove," Cowher said. "We played him more than Leroy (Thompson, in the preseason), but we're doing it to answer some questions. We know Leroy is a quality football player. There are some things we're trying to find out about Timmy."

The injury to O'Donnell has temporarily put the offense in Mike Tomczak's control, but either way expect the Steelers to begin the regular season with more passing plays. That's to help counter opposing defenses who were stacking the line of scrimmage to stop Foster at the end of last season.

The Steelers' offensive line has grown from a

Cowher Power

Annie O'Neill

weakness to a strength in less than a year — Dawson and Haselrig made the Pro Bowl and John Jackson is underrated at left tackle — but Cowher does not want to rely on them merely to clear holes for Foster.

"We want to become more efficient in the whole realm of things and not just focus on running the ball," Cowher said. "We want to have the ability to throw it if they're going to sit there in an eight-man front. But we don't want to lose sight of the fact that what we do best is run the football."

The Steelers have several changes on the defensive line with Gerald Williams moving to end and Joel Steed stepping in at nose tackle, but the biggest overhaul is at linebacker where Levon Kirkland replaces David Little, Jerry Olsavsky replaces Hardy Nickerson and Kevin Greene was signed as a free agent to replace Jerrol Williams.

Cowher talks to his coaches up in the booth from the sideline.

Also, Cowher would like to utilize the talents of No. 2 draft pick Chad Brown and free-agent Reggie Barnes, who has been the hit of training camp. Brown will play as the rush linebacker in the dime defense and Lloyd, who did that last year, will drop into pass coverage, which Nickerson used to do.

"I really think we've upgraded ourselves defensively," Cowher said. "We added a left outside backer (Greene) who is a great complement to our right outside linebacker. When we had Jerrol Williams and Greg Lloyd we had two fast guys who were very good in space, whereas Kevin Greene gives us a degree of more toughness and he's a bigger guy than Jerrol. I feel very good about us defensively and where we are." ✦

1993 Game Of The Year:
Steelers Pay Back Bills

By Ed Bouchette, Post-Gazette Sports Writer

The Steelers last night emphatically staked a claim to the prime turf in the AFC — and buried it smack through the heart of their chief antagonist.

The Buffalo Bills came here with the best record in the NFL and an eight-year winning streak against the Steelers, including two games last season.

It all ended with a crushing, 23-0 victory for the Steelers before 60,265, a regular-season record in Three Rivers Stadium.

The victory moved the Steelers to 6-3 atop the AFC Central Division while the Bills slipped to 7-2.

The Steelers accomplished it all without running back Barry Foster, who left in the first quarter with a sprained ankle. His replacement, Leroy Thompson, gained 108 yards on 30 carries.

Buffalo lost more than a game. Bills quarterback Jim Kelly suffered a concussion late in the first half and did not return. Wide receivers Andre Reed (wrist) and Don Beebe (head) left the game in the second half.

The Steelers made it look easy, scoring in every period. They took a 10-0 halftime lead on Thompson's 9-yard run and a 37-yard Gary Anderson field goal. Eric Green got things going with a 1-yard touchdown pass from Neil O'Donnell and Anderson kicked two more field goals of 19 and 31 yards.

The victory may not have evened the score for the Steelers, who lost to the Bills, 24-3, in the playoffs here last January. But it could go a long way toward some postseason success for them this season.

The Bills, who had beaten the Steelers five straight times, appeared to be steaming toward their fourth AFC Championship.

Last night, all that might have changed.

The Steelers jumped on top 7-0 on Thompson's 9-yard run with 5:31 left in the first quarter. It capped a convincing first drive by the Steelers of 81 yards on 15 plays, taking seven minutes and 17 seconds.

Thompson entered the game after Foster sprained his left ankle in the middle of the drive when linebacker Mark Maddox broke up a screen pass to him.

Thompson carried three straight times of 3, 6 and 9 yards for the TD. On the scoring run, he dashed up the middle, cut deftly to his left and ran into the end zone without a hand ever touching him.

The Steelers made it 2-for-3 when they put together another scoring drive on their third try, ending in Anderson's 37-yard field goal and a 10-0 lead with 9:14 left in the first half.

Buffalo, meanwhile, could go nowhere in the first half until a last-minute surprise. The Bills' first six drives began at their 20 or less, and they did not get beyond their own 45 in the first five.

They were backed up to their own 18 with a third-and-10 and 44 seconds on the clock when Kelly went deep to Andre Reed. Cornerback Rod Woodson was on Reed, but he appeared to lose the ball and the receiver. Reed caught it for a 51-yard gain, and the Bills set up shop on the Steelers' 31.

Two plays later, defensive end Kenny Davidson saved three points for the Steelers by sacking Kelly for an 11-yard loss back to the 40. With time running out, Kelly then threw incomplete on the final play, and the Steelers gladly took their 10-point lead to the locker room.

The Bills were able to get to O'Donnell for three sacks in the first half. That's as many sacks as the Steelers had allowed in their previous five ballgames.

Also, Merril Hoge had a carry in the first half of 24 yards, just three yards fewer than he had gained all season.

The Steelers did a good job controlling the ball in the first half. They held it for 20:25 compared to just 9:35 for the Bills. The Steelers also converted seven of 11 third-down plays in the first two quarters compared to just 2-for-8 for the Bills.

The third quarter looked a whole lot like the first two.

The Steelers took the opening drive and went 70 yards for a touchdown. O'Donnell passed to Dwight Stone for 20 of those. Ernie Mills then took a handoff from Thompson and scooted 19 more.

Green, having another monster game, caught a 14-yard pass to the one. O'Donnell then faked a handoff to Thompson, rolled right and hit a wide-open Green in the right corner of the end zone for a touchdown that made it 17-0 Steelers.

In addition to being good, the Steelers were lucky as well.

Tight end Adrian Cooper, playing for the first time since Oct. 24, caught a 38-yard pass to the Buffalo 14. On third down, safety Mark Kelso intercepted an O'Donnell pass on the goal line. But defensive end Oliver Barnett crushed O'Donnell after the play and was penalized for roughing the passer.

That gave the ball back to the Steelers, and they wound up with a 19-yard Anderson field goal for a 20-0 bulge.

In that third quarter alone, the Steelers held the ball for 11:47 to just 3:13 for Buffalo.

Anderson added a 31-yard field goal in the fourth quarter for a 23-0 lead. ✦

Cowher Power

REGULAR SEASON (9-7)

Date	Visitor		Home		Date	Visitor		Home	
9/5/93	49ers	24	Steelers	13	11/15/93	Bills	0	Steelers	23
9/12/93	Steelers	0	Rams	27	11/21/93	Steelers	13	Broncos	37
9/19/93	Bengals	7	Steelers	34	11/28/93	Steelers	3	Oilers	23
9/27/93	Steelers	45	Falcons	17	12/5/93	Patriots	14	Steelers	17
10/10/93	Chargers	3	Steelers	16	12/13/93	Steelers	21	Dolphins	20
10/17/93	Saints	14	Steelers	37	12/19/93	Oilers	26	Steelers	17
10/24/93	Steelers	23	Browns	28	12/26/93	Steelers	6	Seahawks	16
11/7/93	Steelers	24	Bengals	16	1/2/94	Browns	9	Steelers	16

PLAYOFFS

Date	Visitor		Home	
1/8/94	Steelers	24	Chiefs	27

INDIVIDUAL STATS

PASSING

Name	CMP	ATT	PCT	YDs	YPC	TDs	INTs	Sacks	Rating
O'Donnell	270	486	56	3208	11.9	14	7	41	79.5
Tomczak	29	54	54	398	13.7	2	5	7	51.3

KICKING

Name	XP	XPA	FG	FGA	Points
Anderson	32	32	28	30	116

PUNTING

Name	att	avg	Inside 20
Royals	89	43	28

RUSHING

Name	ATT	YDS	AVG	TDs
Hoge	205	763	4	3
Foster	177	711	4	8
Hoge	51	249	5	1
Stone	12	121	10	1
O'Donnell	26	111	4	0
Worley	10	33	3	0
Mills	3	12	4	0
Cuthbert	1	7	7	0
Jones	10	0	0	0
Tomczak	5	-4	-1	0

RECEIVING

Name	REC	YDS	AVG	TDs
Green	63	942	15	5
Stone	41	587	14	2
Graham	38	579	15	0
Mills	29	386	13	1
Thompson	38	259	7	0
Hoge	33	247	8	4
Foster	27	217	8	1
Thigpen	9	154	17	3
Cooper	9	112	12	0
Davenport	4	51	13	0
Hastings	3	44	15	0
Worley	3	13	4	0
Jorden	1	12	12	0
Cuthbert	1	3	3	0

INTERCEPTIONS

Name	INT
Woodson	8
Perry	4
Lake	4
Johnson	3
Woodson	2
Nickerson	1
Williams	1
Figures	1
Williams	1
Davidson	1

SACKS

Name	Sacks
Greene	12
Lloyd	6
Evans	6
Lake	5
Brown	3
Woodson	2
Steed	2
Davidson	2
Nickerson	1
Kirkland	1
Williams	1
Henry	1

Back To Basics
Steelers can make noise if Foster, defense sound

By Ed Bouchette, Post-Gazette Sports Writer

Reporters simply are no match for the Steelers' Barry Foster when he does not want to talk.

Many times, Foster can freeze his pursuer with a mere look and a wave of his arm.

His injured left ankle may be close to normal, but he is in midseason form avoiding interviews in the Steelers' locker room.

"Get away; I have nothing to say," Foster said, waving his arm up and down.

The Steelers can only hope that he is as successful running over NFL defenses again as he does reporters. When he feels well, so do they. Their offense has centered on his many powerful bursts through the line the past two seasons, and plans call for it again when the Steelers open the 1994 campaign against Dallas at Three Rivers Stadium next Sunday.

Foster rushed for 1,690 yards in 1992 and the Steelers went 11-5, the best record in the American Conference. He was on his way to another fine season in 1993, when he injured his ankle in the ninth game, against Buffalo. He finished with 711 yards rushing, and the Steelers went 3-5 without him to go 9-7 and lose their playoff game.

They have a few new weapons on offense this season, most notably rookie wide receiver Charles Johnson and fullback John L. Williams. But, to steal an old boast from Bubby Brister, Barry's the

man, write it down, and the Steelers need a big year from him in order to do anything.

"No question," said backfield coach Dick Hoak. "Any team would need a big year from your running back. Last year, we were fortunate. He was having a good year when he was hurt."

As Hoak pointed out, the team still got nearly 1,500 yards from the halfback spot because Leroy Thompson filled in and led the Steelers with 763 yards rushing.

But Thompson's yards were quite different than Foster's. They were softer, produced by a finesse runner. Foster has all the finesse of a jackhammer, and his constant pounding wears down a defense.

"He's a strong guy," Hoak said, "and as the game goes on, people get tired and he doesn't get tired very easily. He's in good shape, and he's a strong person."

The Steelers need that again, those 30-carry games that not only produce yards and first downs, but keep drives going, keep the ball away from the other team and wear down defenses. Their record is 20-4 the past two seasons when a back carried more than 20 times a game, including 4-0 when Thompson did it in 1993.

Thompson was traded this summer to New England, and rookie Bam Morris and Randy Cuthbert will back up Foster.

Cowher Power

Neil O'Donnell's 18-yard touchdown [pass to Andre Hastings with 10:04 remaining. put the Steelers up 7-3, and John L. Willimas short scoring run a few minutes later wrapped up the victory.

Peter Diana

Hoak, Coach Bill Cowher and Foster all believe his ankle will be able to sustain such punishment.

"I think he's on schedule," Cowher said. "I'm sure to his own admission, he's still gaining confidence. I think he got a little bit of it (against Indianapolis, Aug. 20). I think Barry is fine. I think he's right where he needs to be.

"Confidence is a very important part of it. I think he has a lot of confidence, he's taking some hits, he's made some cuts."

In that third exhibition game against the Colts, Foster carried 13 times for just 35 yards and went down easily a few times, something that's rarely seen.

"He was a little rusty," Hoak explained. "You know, he only played half of last season and he really hasn't worked that much at training camp live. I think he's a little rusty and I think he'll even admit that to you."

Ray Seals tackles LeRoy Hoard in the first match-up of the season with the Browns.

What about it, Barry?

"Get away."

Foster has talked to reporters after games for the most part this year, but maintains the cold shoulder during the week. They often get the same response the team's medical staff received when they recommended he not have surgery on his ankle — Foster turned his back on them.

Safety Gary Jones, however, has seen a different side of him. Both are from the Dallas area and they golfed together once or twice a week in the off-season. It is a game Foster recently took up to fill the hours in which he is not fishing for bass.

"He's straight-up; there's no fake side to Barry," said Jones. "What you see is what you get. He

Darrell Sapp

doesn't let many people into his inner circle. You just have to understand the type of person he is and what he represents."

Foster is stubborn, as the Steelers have discovered through two renegotiated contracts and one dispute over an ankle injury. Yet through all his problems, he has never stirred up trouble in the locker room, and certainly has not caused any off-field problems. On the field, he is all business and rarely does he show off.

Away from the team, he rarely goes out at night.

"He's to himself, in a good way," said wide receiver Dwight Stone, who knows Foster as well as any of his teammates can. "You never see him hanging out in bars."

Nothing about the NFL or his celebrity overwhelms him.

"I've been around a lot of guys," said Hoak, who played for the Steelers in the 1960s and coached here since 1972. "He was one of the more mature players I ever saw come into this league. A lot of kids come here and they're not quite ready for this. He knew how to handle everything, probably because of his upbringing, his father leaving him and all that. He was always on an even keel."

Gary Jones, the Steelers' outgoing safety, says he probably gets along with Foster so well because they have such different personalities.

"Barry is a litle different than people see in here," he said, sweeping his hand around the Steelers' locker room. "In here, he's secluded. But he has a good business mind, and he does things with guys he's close to.

Peter Diana

"I don't think (publicity) is important to him. He has a lot of goals he set for himself, and they're on the field. I don't know if what comes along with it is important to him — the fame part. I think he's more comfortable just being one of the guys."

That's exactly what he is not on the field, and what he cannot be if the Steelers are to achieve the lofty goals they have this season. They need the Foster of 1992, the kind of running back Hoak believes has few equals in the NFL.

"Barry is strong and has exceptional quickness,"

Barry Foster breaks into the secondary.

he said. "A lot of backs, when they're making a cut, you can knock them off their feet. Barry is so strong, he doesn't get knocked off his feet. He's a strong guy who can break tackles and he also has quickness and speed.

"I think he's one of the better running backs in the league, when he's healthy."

The Steelers can only hope he is, and that he stays that way. ✦

1994 Game Of The Year:
Struck by lightning
Championship fades just three yards away

By Ed Bouchette, Post-Gazette Sports Writer

Welcome to Pfffffftsburgh!

The air you heard rushing out of rainy Three Rivers Stadium was not caused by a blitzing Steelers defense, but by the large hole punctured in their Super Bowl balloon.

The underdog and overwhelmed San Diego Chargers found a way to prick the Steelers' defense for three big plays to steal a 17-13 victory in the American Football Conference championship game yesterday.

It was the first time the Steelers lost the AFC title at home since 1972, and sent San Diego on to its first Super Bowl, in Miami on Jan. 29.

The Steelers crushed the Chargers on the stat sheet with 415 yards to San Diego's 226. But they blew a 13-3 third-quarter lead and their dominance could not help them score, including the final drive that ended when Neil O'Donnell's fourth-down pass from the 3 to Barry Foster in the end zone was knocked down by linebacker Dennis Gibson with 1:04 left.

"Had we been shut out," said Steelers offensive coordinator Ron Erhardt, "or nothing happened on offense, you'd say you don't deserve it. But when you dominate a team the way we did offensively, it's discouraging, it's disgusting not to be in the big one."

Some players had trouble swallowing the results as well.

Cornerback Tim McKyer was beaten by wide receiver Tony Martin for the winning touchdown pass with 5:13 left, a perfect 43-yard heave by quarterback Stan Humphries. A distraught McKyer had to be helped off the field and into the Steelers locker room by two men after the game. He slumped at his locker and declined to talk about it.

"I'm sure everyone in our locker room is very hurt," safety Carnell Lake said, "and it's going to hurt for a long time."

"To me," linebacker Chad Brown said, "it's almost like a dream."

The Chargers, though, became the Steelers' worst nightmare. Few gave the AFC West champs much chance against the team with the best record in the conference, playing at home and playing at its peak. San Diego players said little all week about the Steelers' plans to cut a Super Bowl video and about their boasts that the Chargers would not score.

"I wonder what these guys are going to do with their Super Bowl video now," free safety Stanley Richard said. "Maybe we need to get their coordinator over to San Diego so we can get our video going."

If the Steelers could cut a few scenes out of yesterday's video, they might have something.

"Three plays they made," Lake said, "and three plays we didn't make. In big games like this, it's what it's going to come down to."

Their offense came out smoking, unlike anything they've seen in a long time. They were unable to run, managing just 66 yards, so they passed -- and passed and passed. O'Donnell set AFC championship game records with 54 passing attempts and 32 completions, and set a Steelers postseason record with 349 yards.

All that, and O'Donnell was not intercepted and was not sacked.

"You could throw for 550 yards and it doesn't matter unless you win," a dejected O'Donnell said.

He directed the Steelers' offense to a score on the opening drive as a record 61,545 fans in gloomy Three Rivers Stadium roared their approval. O'Donnell snapped off a 16-yard pass to fullback John L. Williams for a 7-0 lead with 7:28 left in the first quarter.

But the Steelers then blew some scoring opportunities and allowed the Chargers to stay in the game, as the NFL's best running game failed them at crucial times.

"We were trying to run the ball," Erhardt said. "We needed more yardage with the runs. I was a little concerned we didn't get the run going. But the pass was working beautifully, so we kept using it."

They were perched with a first down on the San Diego 27 in the second quarter when Foster ripped around right end. Guard Duval Love, though, was called for holding on the play — one of three holding penalties against the Steelers. That pushed them back to the 37 and when they managed only to reach the 34, they punted.

Then came one of San Diego's Big Three.

Humphries dropped back from the Steelers' 48 and threw into the end zone for Shawn Jefferson, who got slightly behind cornerback Deon Figures.

Figures yanked Jefferson and was called for pass interference. The penalty gave the Chargers a first down at the 2, but three Natrone Means cracks into the line lost a yard thanks to linebacker Levon Kirkland.

The Chargers settled for a 20-yard John Carney field goal, cutting their deficit to 7-3.

The Steelers responded with another long drive, but after getting to the 12, tackle Leon Searcy was whistled for holding and they settled for Gary Anderson's 39-yard field goal nine seconds before the half, which ended with the Steelers on top, 10-3.

Again, on their first drive of the third quarter, the Steelers scored after Rod Woodson intercepted Humphries to give them the ball at the Chargers' 44.

They got to the 6, where they had a first down. But Foster got nothing, O'Donnell threw incomplete twice and Anderson came on to kick a 23-yard field goal to make what seemed like a safe 13-3 lead with 10:37 left in the third quarter.

"I thought from the get-go we had the game won," said wide receiver Andre Hastings, "from the time we stepped on the field, to the first touchdown, all the way down to the time they scored."

But along came Big Play Two.

With a first down at the Steelers' 43, Humphries faked a handoff to Means. Figures bit on the run and tight end Alfred Pupunu ran past him and into the wide-open spaces of the Steelers' secondary. Humphries hit Pupunu at the 20 and he ran it in for a touchdown that cut the Steelers' lead to 13-10 with 8:23 left in the third quarter.

"When the tight end down-blocks and the guard and tackle pull around, that's about as run-read as you can get," said Lake, who came up to fill the gap.

The Steelers still led, but the large crowd could sense the uncomfortable change in momentum.

The Chargers began their winning drive on their 20 with 9:57 left in the game. They reached the Steelers' 38, but on third down, a false start pushed them back to the 43, making it third-and-14.

Humphries dropped back and threw deep just before he was crushed by Brown. Martin had beaten McKyer by a step and rookie safety Boo Bell was late providing help. The pass was perfect and Martin caught it at the goal line.

"Timmy just had a bad read," cornerback Woodson said. "Timmy just lost his guy and Stan just threw the ball a mile in the air. I don't have any hard feelings toward Timmy. I don't think anybody does."

McKyer was tougher on himself than anybody. Ironically, Figures sat next to him trying to console him at his locker. Later, Cowher and defensive coordinator Dom Capers were talking to him in their offices.

But the Steelers had one last chance to pull it out.

With 5:02 left, they got the ball on their own 17. O'Donnell threw seven straight passes and completed all seven, the last one a 21-yard pickup to tight end Eric Green to the San Diego 9.

The Steelers seemed to be in great shape with two minutes left and a first down.

A draw to Foster lost a yard. Gibson knocked away a pass to Green. O'Donnell then threw over the middle to Williams. The pass did not hit him in stride, but he picked up 7 yards to the 3.

"If he gets it in stride, he might score," Erhardt said.

That left fourth down from the 3. The Steelers called time to discuss the play. They sent four receivers out. Green was double-teamed. Foster flashed open ever so slightly over the middle in the end zone. O'Donnell threw low and as Foster reached to grab it, Gibson knocked it down with one hand.

"You just sit down and hope it works out," Woodson said of the final play. "But the majority of time, it doesn't work out that way."

Humphries then ran three keepers to run out the final 1:04.

"Seeing that clock tick down," said Steelers wide receiver Ernie Mills, "is all I can think about right now."

They will have a long off-season to do so. ✦

Cowher Power

REGULAR SEASON (12-4)

Date	Visitor		Home		Date	Visitor		Home	
9/4/94	Cowboys	26	Steelers	9	11/6/94	Steelers	12	Oilers	9*
9/11/94	Steelers	17	Browns	10	11/14/94	Bills	10	Steelers	23
9/18/94	Colts	21	Steelers	31	11/20/94	Dolphins	13	Steelers	16*
9/25/94	Steelers	13	Seahawks	30	11/27/94	Steelers	21	Raiders	3
10/3/94	Oilers	14	Steelers	30	12/4/94	Steelers	38	Bengals	15
10/16/94	Bengals	10	Steelers	14	12/11/94	Eagles	3	Steelers	14
10/23/94	Steelers	10	Giants	6	12/18/94	Browns	7	Steelers	17
10/30/94	Steelers	17	Cardinals	20*	12/24/94	Steelers	34	Chargers	37

*OT

PLAYOFFS

Date	Visitor		Home	
1/7/95	Browns	9	Steelers	29
1/15/95	Chargers	17	Steelers	13

INDIVIDUAL STATS

PASSING

Date	Visitor		Home	
1/7/95	Browns	9	Steelers	29
1/15/95	Chargers	17	Steelers	13

KICKING

Name	XP	XPA	FG	FGA	Points
Anderson	32	32	24	29	104

PUNTING

Name	att	avg	Inside 20
Royals	97	40	35

RUSHING

Name	ATT	YDS	AVG	TDs
Foster	216	851	4	5
Williams	198	836	4	7
Morris	68	317	5	1
O'Donnell	31	80	3	1
McAfee	16	56	4	1
Tomczak	4	22	6	0
Mills	3	18	6	0
Stone	2	7	4	0
Avery	2	4	2	0
Anderson	1	3	0	0
Thigpen	4	-1	1	0
Royals	1	-13	-1	0

RECEIVING

Name	REC	YDS	AVG	TDs
Green	46	618	13	4
Johnson	38	577	15	3
Thigpen	36	546	15	4
Mills	19	384	20	1
Williams	51	378	7	2
Hastings	20	281	14	2
Morris	22	204	9	0
Foster	20	124	6	0
Stone	7	81	12	0
Hayes	5	50	10	0
Keith	1	2	2	0
Avery	1	2	2	0

INTERCEPTIONS

Name	INT
Woodson	7
Figures	4
Brown	2
Jones	1
Lake	1
Kirkland	1
Lloyd	1

SACKS

Name	Sacks
Greene	14
Kirkland	10
Lloyd	8
Williams	7
Figures	3
Brown	3
Gildon	2
Buckner	2
Steed	2
Seals	2
McKyer	1
Lake	1

1995

Curtain Call
Steelers defense is the showstopper and the best in the NFL
By Ed Bouchette, Post-Gazette Sports Writer

You could look across the practice field at St. Vincent College, up past the drooping willow trees, and see nothing. The stately Laurel Mountains, quite evident earlier in training camp, vanished behind the steam rising from the valley.

When the mountains disappear, football players know they are in for a miserable, stinking hot afternoon of practice. It was Aug. 15, the most miserable of a miserably hot training camp for the Steelers.

The heat index hit 106 on the practice field that afternoon, the highest recorded in training camp. And after a sweltering, two-hour practice in pads, the Steelers could not wait for a cold shower and a meal.

Well, some could. On their own, the entire starting defense headed for a steep hill that flanks the practice field and 15, 16 of them began running up and down, up and down. Several times they did this before calling it a day. It was the first day in training camp for safety Carnell Lake and it was as if they were waiting for him so they could make a statement together, as a complete unit, as an example to everyone that they don't intend to come up short again this season.

"They understand that this is the standard," linebacker Greg Lloyd said of his defensive teammates, old and new. "This is the standard for everybody, not just the starters."

Last season, the Steelers defense finished 15 yards short of the No. 1- ranking in the NFL and one big play of landing in the Super Bowl. They have no intentions of missing either this season. They believe they are the best defense in football and will shine a light on the path to the Super Bowl this time.

Smack in the middle of the era of free agency, the Steelers have been able to keep intact their Blitzburgh defense. Every starter from last season returns, although Deon Figures will not open the season at cornerback because of the bullet wound he suffered in May. Four made the Pro Bowl — Lloyd, Greene, Lake and cornerback Rod Woodson. But that doesn't begin to tell the story how good their defense is.

It is a defense that led the NFL last season with 55 quarterback sacks and finished No. 2 overall in yardage allowed, just 15 yards more than Dallas. They permitted the fewest touchdowns of any defense in the NFL — 19.

Those are the cold, hard facts. It gets more subjective when soliciting opinions about which defense is the best in the NFL. It also is difficult finding objective opinions about it. But it is hard to find anyone these days who does not think the Steelers have the best.

"If they stay on the same line they were last year

Bill Wade

— and there's no reason why they wouldn't — I think they would have to be the defense right now, overall," said John Wooten, a longtime NFL player personnel man.

"I'm talking about the run, pass coverage, sacks, blitzing — the whole package. They can do it all."

Another NFC personnel man, who asked not to be identified, mentally clicked through the top defenses in the league. He came to the same conclusion as Wooten.

"Green Bay came on at the end of last season, but

Neil O'Donnell and his wife are escorted from Sun Devil Stadium by security following the Super Bowl XXX loss to the Dallas Cowboys.

they lost Bryce Paup. The Vikings are good against the run, but their secondary is suspect. The 49ers are overrated. They have no outside rushers. Cleveland is pretty good. Miami will be helped by Trace Armstrong and Steve Emtman.

"But I'd have to say the Steelers are the best. And their linebackers are exceptional." ✦

1995 Game Of The Year:

Thumbs Up

This time, the bounce in the end zone goes the Steelers' way

By Ed Bouchette, Post-Gazette Sports Writer

Franco Harris was there, on the Steelers' sideline, as was Kordell Stewart. They know a little about creating miracle football endings, but this time they could only watch and wait as Jim Harbaugh's prayer on the last play of the AFC championship was launched from the 29 toward the goal line.

Indianapolis receivers and Steelers defensive backs packed into the end zone like bachelors waiting for the garter toss. The stakes: a trip to the Super Bowl.

"It seemed like it took forever," Steelers safety Darren Perry said. "You could just see this big ball. It looked huge and it looked like it was coming in slow motion."

And after Perry tipped it and others swiped at it, the ball came right down into the lap of Colts wide receiver Aaron

Bailey on the ground. He seemed to have it, but the ball rolled off his chest, onto the turf, the officials ruled it incomplete and the Steelers were going to the Super Bowl.

"It was," Bailey moaned, "almost another Immaculate Reception."

But close didn't count for the Horseshoes, as Bailey's non-catch on the final play and Ernie Mills' game-winning 37-yard reception with 1:51 left propelled the Steelers to a 20-16 victory over the Colts in the AFC championship.

The game had everything that last year's title game had with two big differences. The favored Steelers won this time and they came from behind to do it.

"Maybe it was poetic justice," said Steelers Coach Bill Cowher, who had tears in his eyes after the biggest win of his career. "Having been there again with the ball in the air and an opportunity to win a championship. Now I'm 1-1. It was a great feeling."

It finally erased the memories of last year's upset loss to San Diego in the title game and puts the Steelers in the Super Bowl for the first time in 16 years. They will play Dallas, a team they beat in Super Bowls X and XIII.

"When I saw the ref go like this," said Steelers defensive end Ray Seals, waving his hands, "it was over, baby. Cinderella's gone. We're in."

Indianapolis, though, played more like Godzilla than the 11-point underdogs that the Colts were. They scored on three Cary Blanchard field goals, one in each quarter, and trailed 13-9 in the fourth only because of a disputed touchdown reception by the Steelers' Kordell Stewart to go with two

Steelers and Colts players pray at midfield following Pittsburgh's victory in the AFC Championship game at Three Rivers Stadium in 1996.

Peter Diana

The Steelers defense kept Jim Harbaugh and his Colts in check for most of the game.

Norm Johnson field goals.

Then Harbaugh silenced the 61,062 at Three Rivers Stadium like no one since Stan Humphries and Tony Martin of San Diego. He beat a Steelers blitz and lofted a 47-yard touchdown pass to Floyd Turner to put Indy on top 16-13 with 8:46 left and the Steelers were being haunted again.

"Yeah," Seals admitted, "it was in the back of your mind, 'Damn, is this going to happen to us again?' But last year we

didn't finish. This year, we pulled it out and that's the difference in this team."

They put together some magic of their own before and during their winning touchdown drive.

The Steelers reached the 50 but could not convert a third-and-5 on their next series and punted to Indy with 6:29 left. The Colts' Lamont Warren fumbled on the first play from the 9 but guard Joe Staysniak recovered and the break the Steelers needed had just eluded them.

On third-and-1, however, with 3:57 left, the Steelers created their own break — with a broken play on defense. Warren took a handoff and headed left. Safety Myron Bell was supposed to blitz on the play but did not. Seeing this, cornerback Willie Williams dashed in from the opposite side, sliced through the Colts backfield and brought Warren down by the ankles for no gain.

"I saw Harbaugh give the ball off to Lamont and I just had to make the tackle," Williams said. "If I didn't make the tackle he probably would have made first down and it would have been a different ballgame."

Instead of keeping a clock-killing drive going, the Colts had to punt and Andre Hastings returned it 12 yards to the 33.

With 3:03 left, quarterback Neil O'Donnell began a drive that had the looks of last year's that ended 3 yards short against San Diego. He threw to Stewart for 13 and to John L. Williams for 7. He then nearly threw the game away when his pass for Mills went straight into the hands of linebacker Quintin Coryatt. But Coryatt dropped it after Mills swiped his left arm.

"I thought he had the ball and I just swung my arm and tried to hit it and knock it out," Mills said. "If he catches it, it's over."

They faced sudden death two plays later, on fourth-and-3 with barely two minutes to go. O'Donnell, not having one of his best days, came up big at the end. He slipped a 9-yard pass to Andre Hastings for a first down.

"They lost me in the shuffle and Neil made a great throw," Hastings said. "I think he threw it between three guys and hit me in the numbers." ✦

REGULAR SEASON (11-5)

Date	Visitor		Home		Date	Visitor		Home	
9/3/95	Lions	20	Steelers	23	11/5/95	Steelers	37	Bears	34*
9/10/95	Steelers	34	Oilers	17	11/13/95	Browns	3	Steelers	20
9/18/95	Steelers	10	Dolphins	23	11/19/95	Steelers	49	Bengals	31
9/24/95	Vikings	44	Steelers	24	11/26/95	Steelers	20	Browns	17
10/1/95	Chargers	16	Steelers	31	12/3/95	Oilers	7	Steelers	21
10/8/95	Steelers	16	Jaguars	20	12/10/95	Steelers	29	Raiders	10
10/19/95	Bengals	27	Steelers	9	12/16/95	Patriots	27	Steelers	41
10/29/95	Jaguars	7	Steelers	24	12/24/95	Steelers	19	Packers	24

*OT

PLAYOFFS

Date	Visitor		Home	
11/6/96	Bills	21	Steelers	40
1/14/96	Colts	16	Steelers	20
1/28/96	Cowboys	27	Steelers	17

INDIVIDUAL STATS

PASSING

Name	CMP	ATT	PCT	YDs	YPC	TDs	INTs	Sacks	Rating
O'Donnell	246	416	59	2970	12.1	17	7	15	87.7
Tomczak	65	113	58	666	10.2	1	9	6	44.3
Miller	32	56	57	397	12.4	2	5	2	53.9
Stewart	5	7	71	60	12	1	0	1	136.9

KICKING

Name	XP	XPA	FG	FGA	Points
Johnson	39	39	34	41	141

PUNTING

Name	att	avg	Inside 20
Stark	59	40	20

RUSHING

Name	ATT	YDS	AVG	TDs
Pegram	213	813	4	5
Morris	148	559	4	9
McAfee	39	156	4	1
Williams	29	110	4	0
Stewart	15	86	6	1
O'Donnell	24	45	2	0
Mills	5	39	8	0
Tomczak	11	25	2	0
Hastings	1	14	14	0
Lester	5	9	2	1
Avery	1	3	3	0
Miller	1	2	2	0
Thigpen	1	1	1	0
Johnson	1	-10	-1	0

RECEIVING

Name	REC	YDS	AVG	TDs
Thigpen	85	1307	15	5
Mills	39	679	17	8
Hastings	48	502	11	1
Johnson	38	432	11	0
Bruener	26	238	9	3
Stewart	14	235	17	1
Pegram	26	206	8	1
Williams	24	127	5	1
Hayes	11	113	10	0
McAfee	15	88	6	0
Avery	11	82	8	1
Barnes	3	48	16	0
Morris	8	36	5	0

INTERCEPTIONS

Name	INT
Williams	7
Perry	4
Lloyd	3
Figures	2
Bell	2
Mays	2
Oldham	1
Lake	1
Greene	1
Seals	1

SACKS

Name	Sacks
Greene	9
Seals	8
Lloyd	6
Brown	6
Gildon	3
Buckner	3
Lake	2
Henry	2
Kirkland	1
Olsavsky	1
Steed	1

Star Struck

Dallas holds off Steelers rally and extends AFC's losing streak

By Ed Bouchette, Post-Gazette Sports Writer

The Dallas Cowboys had to sweat for it, but they emerged yesterday as a dynasty in mid-stream and the Steelers helped with their coronation.

Dallas won an unprecedented third Super Bowl in four years by holding off the Steelers for a 27-17 victory, joining San Francisco as the only teams to win five Lombardi trophies.

The Steelers trailed by just three points with four minutes left before cornerback Larry Brown intercepted his second Neil O'Donnell pass of the second half and returned it 33 yards to the Steelers' 6. Emmitt Smith then ran it in for a 4-yard touchdown with 3:43 left that ended the Steelers' comeback from 13 points down in the first half.

While they made an exciting game of it, the underdog Steelers became the 12th straight AFC team to fall victim in the Super Bowl and it was their first loss in the championship in five tries.

"It's been one great run," Steelers Coach Bill Cowher said. "We didn't get to the top of the mountain, but it was a great run along the way."

The Steelers' comeback brought a gracious response from Cowboys owner Jerry Jones at the trophy presentation.

"I want to tell all you Steelers fans ... what a team you have and what a ballgame."

Both of Brown's interceptions led to Dallas touchdowns, their only scores of the second half. He picked one off midway through the third quarter and returned it 44 yards that led to a 1-yard TD run by Smith.

Brown's two big plays earned him the game's MVP award, the first by a cornerback ever in the Super Bowl and the first defensive back so honored since safety Jake Scott of Miami in Super Bowl VII.

O'Donnell also threw a third interception on a desperation pass on the last play of the game. Those were the only turnovers in the Super Bowl. Cowher said the first interception resulted because the ball sailed on O'Donnell — no receiver was anywhere near it — but that the second occurred because of a miscommunication between O'Donnell and his receiver, Andre Hastings.

"The bottom line is two big plays," Cowher said. "We couldn't get a turnover and they had the turnovers and that's the difference sometimes.

"Neil got us here. Without Neil O'Donnell, we wouldn't be playing the last of January. I told him to look at the big picture and not the final piece."

O'Donnell threw just seven interceptions all season. Yesterday, he completed 28 of 49 passes for 239 yards and was sacked four times.

"It's not characteristic of Neil O'Donnell," the quarterback said. "It's just too bad we fell a little short because we had an opportunity to win it."

John Beale

Carnell Lake is upended as Michael Irvin hauls in a first-half reception.

Troy Aikman to tight end Jay Novacek. Neil O'Donnell threw a 6-yard scoring pass to Yancey Thigpen 13 seconds before halftime for the Steelers, who got scores in the second half when Norm Johnson kicked a 46-yard field goal and Bam Morris ran over from the 1 with 6:36 left in the game to put them within three.

That last touchdown came after the Steelers converted an onside kick with 11:20 left and trailing by 10. Johnson kicked off short to the right sideline and Deon Figures scooped it up at the Steelers' 48.

Kordell Stewart moved behind center to convert a fourth-and-1 at the Steelers' 49 in the first quarter but they weren't so lucky on two third-quarter calls.

"We came here to win the game, not to play to lose," Cowher said. "Those fourth-down calls, any one of them, I would do again. If I had to do it again, I would do every one of them."

Morris outgained Smith, 73 yards to 49. Aikman, though, outperformed O'Donnell by completing 15 of 23 passes for 209 yards and the biggest stat of the Super Bowl — no interceptions. Levon Kirkland and Ray Seals each had a sack of Aikman and Chad Hennings had two of the Cowboys' four sacks of O'Donnell.

Hastings of the Steelers also led all receivers with 10 catches for 98 yards and Ernie Mills had eight for 78. Michael Irvin led the Cowboys with five catches for 76 yards.

The Steelers outgained Dallas, 310 yards to 254.

"Pittsburgh played a great ballgame the whole day," Smith said. "I have a lot of respect for them. They just started coming at us and kept coming. They never quit. They never let down. And fortunately we made enough plays to win the game." ✦

Without Brown's interceptions, the Steelers probably would have won the game. After a shaky start and a 13-0 deficit midway through the second quarter, they dominated more than half the game on offense and defense, and used a successful onside kick in the fourth quarter to create an opportunity for them to win.

"I'd like to commend Pittsburgh for the way they played," Dallas Coach Barry Switzer said. "They dominated the second half."

Dallas took that 13-0 lead on Chris Boniol field goals of 42 and 35 yards and a 3-yard TD pass from

Cowher Power

Peter Diana

Larry Brown looks upfield after intercepting Neil O'Donnell pass in the fourth quarter.

1996

Thud!
Steelers battered and beaten in opener

By Ed Bouchette, Post-Gazette Sports Writer

Levon Kirkland, one of those rare Steelers linebackers without a knee injury yesterday, looked over the devastation of their locker room and groaned.

"Bad things happen," Kirkland said. "And it happened quickly."

As quick as knee ligaments snapping, the Steelers' defensive prospects turned sour when they lost All-Pro Greg Lloyd for the season and two other outside linebackers for a month or so — starter Jason Gildon and rookie backup Steve Conley.

" 'Season-ending,' " fellow linebacker Jerry Olsavsky said, "are not two words you like to hear."

There was more bad news on their offense even though no one got hurt. All three of their quarterbacks played so poorly that Coach Bill Cowher in essence threw the job open again.

And, finally, the Jacksonville Jaguars pulled off their second stunning win against the Steelers here, 24-9.

"It was kind of hard to find anything good in a game like this," moaned safety Darren Perry.

The Steelers were thunderstruck in their opening game for the second straight year. They lost cornerback Rod Woodson for practically the whole season in 1995 and quarterback Neil O'Donnell for four games with injuries against Detroit at home (a game, at least, that they won).

But this one has a different feel about it, and it's not good. This time, the injuries are piling up. Starting defensive end Ray Seals already was shelved for the season and Woodson continues to struggle back from last year's injury. Their wide receivers are hurting and now they appear to have no No. 1 quarterback.

There was no searching for the problems today. They were obvious," said Steelers linebacker Chad Brown.

It began with poor play from the quarterbacks, who were bouncing passes, overthrowing receivers and doing virtually nothing good all day. Jim Miller reacted to his first NFL start by overthrowing tight end Mark Bruener in the end zone in the second quarter and underthrowing wide receiver Andre Hastings in the end zone in the third quarter.

"Andre was open in the end zone and I'm supposed to hit him. It's as simple as that," said Miller, who missed Bruener because he tried to loft his pass over linebacker Bryan Schwartz, who was underneath and in the line of fire.

The Steelers wound up settling for Norm Johnson field goals of 29 and 23 yards each time after Johnson hit one from 48 yards in the first quarter. That about summed up the Steelers' offense for the day as Miller, Kordell Stewart and Mike Tomczak combined for 86 yards of net passing, one very bad interception by Tomczak and four sacks. Jerome Bettis (57) and Erric Pegram (44) ran well but the

Peter Diana

Steelers running back Jerome Bettis is tackled by Carolina Panthers safety Brett Maxie and Sam Mills in first quarter action.

Peter Diana

Steelers did not commit to their ground game, giving their two backs just 21 carries.

The rest of the afternoon was given over to watching linebackers getting carried off the field and Mark Brunell fooling pass rushers and defensive backs alike.

Brunell, the southpaw Jaguars quarterback more elusive than Kordell Stewart, caught Woodson in a mistake to throw a 38-yard touchdown pass to Willie Jackson in the first period, and hooked up with Keenan McCardell for a 15-yard TD pass in the second over Willie Williams. Brunell wound up with 212 yards passing (20 of 31).

Mike Hollis, who feeds off kicking long field goals against the Steelers, booted one from 52 yards, and James Stewart ran over from the 1 in the final quarter to put the final touches on one of the worst days in recent Steelers history.

"There's no better way to begin the

Jason Gildon prays on the bench during the Steelers final play, which was an interception.

season than to beat the champions," said Jacksonville tackle Leon Searcy, formerly with the Steelers.

And no worse way than to lose to a baby NFL franchise in the opener by 15 points and lose three outside linebacker to boot. Lloyd tore the patella tendon in his left knee. Gildon and Conley sprained their medial collateral ligaments and will be lost an estimated 3-4 weeks, pending MRI exams today.

"He's one of our leaders," defensive coordinator Dick LeBeau said of Lloyd. "He's one of the better players in the league. That's comparable to losing Rod last year."

Overcoming Lloyd's absence may be easier than overcoming O'Donnell's loss this year — to free agency.

Cowher said after the game that he would not

Darrell Sapp

Yancey Thigpen stretches before a November game against the St. Louis Rams.

make a decision on his quarterbacks until this week, and none of the three left him much to choose from. Miller was 9 of 17 for 83 yards and those two misfires. Stewart started the fourth quarter but was yanked when he threw two bad passes. Tomczak was the worst of all when he entered the game in the fourth quarter. He completed three of four passes for 24 yards and was sacked twice.

But it was Tomczak's first pass that ended any hope of a comeback. Trailing 17-9 with 8:13 left, the Steelers got the ball on their 44 after Hastings returned a kickoff 42 yards. On first down, Charles Johnson ran a sideline pattern and Tomczak put the pass right in the hands of rookie linebacker Kevin Hardy. That led to the Jaguars' final TD, Stewart's 1-yard run with 4:49 left.

"We had missed oppportunities on offense, big plays on defense," said Cowher. "Corrections are going to have to be made, are going to be made."

One of those big plays came early with the game scoreless. First, McCardell beat Woodson for a 13-yard reception on Jacksonville's first third-down play of the season. On the last play of that series, Jackson ran a slant over the middle and Woodson was caught short.

Brunell hit Jackson in stride and he ran all the way for a 38-yard touchdown and a 7-0 lead.

"I was playing slant the way our receivers run it," Woodson said. "They run it flat. But their receivers run their slants more up the field and I came underneath and he threw the ball up top like all quarterbacks are supposed to do. After that, it's out the gate."

The gate swung open on another season for the Steelers here yesterday — and it caught them smack under the chin. ✦

Norm Johnson holds the ball after recovering his own on-side kick in the first quarter.

Peter Diana

Cowher Power

Peter Diana

Bill Cowher disputes a call with line judge Jeff Bergman in the 4th quarter of the Steelers' 20-19 loss to the Eagles in Philadelphia.

1996 Game Of The Year:
First Round Knockout
Steelers 42-14 ripping of Colts was best game of the season
By Ed Bouchette, Post-Gazette Sports Writer

The Indianapolis Colts had that Riddick Bowe look about them yesterday. Beaten, bloodied, they kept standing, hanging around, clutching and grabbing and looking for that one miracle opening that would raise their hands at the end.

And, over the span of four minutes near the end of the first half, they got it.

"Anytime you're playing real good football," Rod Woodson said, "'and they're not doing a lot and they're hanging around, sometimes they're going to get a big play somewhere along the line."

They got two of them, really big plays that led to quick touchdowns and a one-point halftime lead for the Colts.

And then the Steelers snapped the door and ran off with a 42-14 rout in the first round of the playoffs at Three Rivers Stadium, scoring four touchdowns in the second half and rushing for 231 yards in the game. It virtually matched their 40-14 blowout of the Colts in the playoffs 20 years ago in Baltimore and produced the most points in their playoff history.

The victory sends the Steelers to Foxboro, Mass., against the AFC East champion New England Patriots Sunday at 12:30 p.m. The winner advances to the conference championship.

"This," Steelers Coach Bill Cowher said, "was one of the better football games we've played in a while. It's something we can feed off of."

Indy quarterback Jim Harbaugh might have trouble eating, period. He chipped two teeth and took at least 15 stitches to his chin when he bit through his lip as linebacker Jason Gildon slammed into him on the fifth play of the game. Harbaugh, though, did not leave the game until the very end, even though he was brutalized the rest of the day by linebacker Chad Brown — who had three sacks — and the rest of the defense.

"I give him lots of credit," said Brown, who continually pressured and knocked down Harbaugh. "It's my job to beat him up, but at the same time I have a lot of respect for him. I told him 'You can play defense for us.' "

Harbaugh got off the turf long enough to throw two big passes after Mike Tomczak threw one in the other direction.

The Steelers held a comfortable 13-0 lead on a Kordell Stewart 1-yard TD run and two Norm Johnson field goals, and they were driving for what seemed like the kill with less than five minutes to go in the half.

Then, on third-and-4 at Indy's 42, Tomczak threw a quick out pass to Ernie Mills near the left sideline.

Cornerback Eugene Daniel, playing tight in a zone, stepped in front of the ball, picked it off and fled 59 yards for a score that silenced the crowd of 58,078 and put the Colts one TD from the lead.

"I wish I had it back," Tomczak said. "I wish I would have thrown it over his head and out of bounds."

"We were a little upset," Woodson said, "because we knew we played very well. We gave up one play on offense and that long pass on defense. We knew we had to regroup and had to take that anger when we came out into the second half."

The Steelers, who for most of the season have had second-half problems, played their best two quarters of 1996.

They went 91 yards on the opening drive on 16 plays in 9fi minutes to score on Jerome Bettis' 1-yard run and took a 21-14 lead when Tomczak found tight end John Farquar for the two-point conversion.

Safety Carnell Lake blitzed from the left and recovered an errant pitch to Marshall Faulk to give the Steelers the ball on the 18 and they made it 28-14 on another Bettis 1-yard run early in the fourth quarter.

Stewart took over for Tomczak and ran 24 yards up the middle on a quarterback draw, then handed off to rookie Jon Witman for a 31-yard touchdown to jump it to 35-14. Finally, Stewart ran 3 yards for his second TD to finish the blowout. ✦

Cowher Power

REGULAR SEASON (10-6)

Date	Visitor		Home		Date	Visitor		Home	
9/1/96	Steelers	9	Jaguars	24	11/3/96	Rams	6	Steelers	42
9/8/96	Ravens	17	Steelers	31	11/10/96	Steelers	24	Bengals	34
9/16/96	Bills	6	Steelers	24	11/17/96	Jaguars	3	Steelers	28
9/29/96	Oilers	16	Steelers	30	11/25/96	Steelers	24	Dolphins	17
10/7/96	Steelers	17	Chiefs	7	12/1/96	Steelers	17	Ravens	31
10/13/96	Bengals	10	Steelers	20	12/8/96	Chargers	3	Steelers	16
10/20/96	Steelers	13	Oilers	23	12/15/96	49ers	25	Steelers	15
10/27/96	Steelers	20	Falcons	17	12/22/96	Steelers	14	Panthers	18

*OT

PLAYOFFS

Date	Visitor		Home	
12/29/96	Colts	14	Steelers	42
1/5/97	Steelers	3	Patriots	28

INDIVIDUAL STATS

PASSING

Name	CMP	ATT	PCT	YDs	YPC	TDs	INTs	Sacks	Rating
Tomczak	222	401	55.4	2767	6.9	15	17	0	71.8
Stewart	11	30	36.7	100	3.3	0	2	0	18.8
Miller	13	25	52	123	4.9	0	0	0	65.9

KICKING

Name	XP	XPA	FG	FGA	Points
Johnson	37	37	23	30	106

PUNTING

Name	att	avg	Inside 20
Miller	55	41	0
Edge	17	39.7	0

RUSHING

Name	ATT	YDS	AVG	TDs
Bettis	320	1431	0	11
Pegram	97	509	1	1
Stewart	38	179	1	5
Hastings	4	71	2	0
Witman	17	69	0	0
Mills	2	24	1	0
Lester	8	20	0	1
Richardson	5	17	0	0
McAfee	7	17	0	0
Arnold	1	-3	0	0
Miller	2	-4	0	0
Tomczak	22	-7	0	0
Edge	1	-16	-2	0

RECEIVING

Name	REC	YDS	AVG	TDs
Johnson	60	1008	16.8	3
Hastings	72	739	10.3	6
Stewart	17	293	17.2	3
Thigpen	12	244	20.3	2
Bruener	12	141	11.8	0
Bettis	22	122	5.5	0
Pegram	17	112	6.6	0
Mills	7	92	13.1	1
Arnold	6	76	12.7	0
Lester	7	70	10	0
Botkin	4	36	9	0
McAfee	5	21	4.2	0
Witman	2	15	7.5	0
Hayes	2	14	7	0
Holliday	1	7	7	0

INTERCEPTIONS

Name	INT
Woodson	6
Perry	5
Kirkland	4
Brown	2
Williams	1
Olsavsky	1
Lake	1
Fuller	1

SACKS

Name	Sacks
Brown	13
Gildon	7
Kirkland	4
Buckner	3
Ravotti	2
Emmons	2
Oldham	2
Gibson	2
Lake	2
Henry	2
Bell	2
Eight players with 1 sack	

1997

Exacting Change

It's another season of challenges for the Steelers who keep finding ways to fill deep holes

By Ed Bouchette, Post-Gazette Sports Writer

But this year there's a new twist in the tale. Two wood doors swing open so often to the lobby of the Steelers' offices it's a wonder the hinges still work. No doorway in the National Football League has gotten such a workout as that at Three Rivers Stadium, where players, coaches and even front office people have left in droves.

Soon, even that entranceway might disappear. If voters approve a referendum in November for an increased sales tax, new football and baseball stadiums would be built and Three Rivers would disappear.

They've been predicting just such a thing for the Steelers since free agency began in 1993. They've been raided of talent like no other team in the NFL, yet keep reappearing in the playoffs each year since 1992, including the past three as AFC Central Division champions.

This year represents not only another challenge to their resiliency, but the team and the franchise finds itself at a crossroads heading into the 21st century.

Free agency cost them more young talent in the months after they defended their AFC Championship by getting blown out of the playoffs in New England. Defensive coordinator Dick LeBeau left for a similar job in Cincinnati amidst reports he did not get along with Coach Bill Cowher, something both men deny. A new starting quarterback, Kordell Stewart, has been installed and he signed a contract that takes

him into the next century.

Nothing, though, may be as important to the Steelers' future as the upcoming vote on the new stadium and various polls have shown the proposal is headed for a resounding defeat at the ballot box.

Revenue from TV and merchandise sales are evenly divided among the NFL's 30 teams, which leaves stadiums as the primary weapon for franchises to make money and gain an edge in luring free agents to play for them. New stadiums are also a means for survival in the new world order of the NFL, because teams are required to pay a certain minimum percentage to their players of the average team's revenue. So, if Dallas produces $35 million more revenue than the Steelers, not only do the Cowboys make more money but they raise the amount the Steelers are required for their payroll.

Sooner or later, it will catch up to them. The four other teams in the AFC Central already have new stadiums or have begun building them, and plans or construction are underway for new stadiums throughout the league, including ones in Seattle, San Francisco, Washington and Cleveland, which does not yet have a team.

New stadiums mean more revenue and without it the exodus of talent will likely continue here.

"We've done well and we're OK right now," Steelers president Dan Rooney said. "But I don't think you can

John Heller

Kordell Stewart discusses strategy with Bill Cowher in a preseason game.

Robin Rombach

be in position to continue to lose players you want."

They lost a bundle in the offseason to free agency — Chad Brown, Rod Woodson, Willie Williams, Ray Seals, Andre Hastings, Ernie Mills, and Deon Figures. They traded halfback Erric Pegram because they could not afford him under the cap. They dumped Jim Miller, their chosen starting quarterback a year ago, because they no longer could afford him. This after losing starting quarterback Neil O'Donnell, tackle Leon Searcy and linebacker Kevin Greene as free agents in 1996.

The Steelers have thrived in the new system, picking up value in free agency, drafting well and keeping a core of their own stars. A case can be made that their toughest loss in free agency, O'Donnell, could turn into a fortunate departure because it paved the way for them to start Stewart.

"The Steelers and Dallas are two teams that lost 20-some players over the past three years," Rooney noted. "But there are players in that number you're just as satisfied they're not with you."

Rooney, his personnel men and Coach Bill Cowher

After scoring his second rushing touchdown of the game against the Broncos, Kordell Stewart is congratulated by Yancey Thigpen.

have not only grasped the new NFL system but have been sharp to recognize and find good talent, and used it correctly. While many teams have tried to figure ways to beat the system, the Steelers have managed to work it to their advantage.

Turnover can be good if those making the decisions know what they're doing.

"From my second year on it seems like we've had a lot of turnover every year," Cowher said.

"It seems every year we have a different team. We have a different quarterback this year; this is the third different quarterback in the last three years. We have a change on defense.

"It's all how you want to perceive it. You can look at it and say it would be nice to have the same guys, then maybe you have some continuity and can pick up where you left off. I've never looked at it as frustrating. That's part of the game. You proba-

Steve Mellon

George Jones is corralled by a gang of Cowboys during the Steelers' season opening loss at Three Rivers Stadium.

bly get more frustrated in February and March and you're watching guys go and there's nothing you can do about it. But by the time you come to camp, you know you're going to have 80 guys and it does no good to dwell on it."

College coaches deal with it annually. Even their best players can only play four seasons. While many have focused on the Steelers losses in free agency, they should get credit for keeping many of their best players here. This is a team that has Dermontti Dawson, Greg Lloyd, Carnell Lake, Levon Kirkland, Jerome Bettis, John Jackson, Will Wolford, Joel Steed, Charles Johnson, Yancey Thigpen and Darren Perry.

Where would they have been had they paid Rod Woodson $3 million a year to stay? They'd be in trouble, that's where. They would not have signed cornerback Donnell Woolford as a free agent and Woodson has had physical problems in San Francisco.

They also would have had less money to sign others.

They have done well warding off the ravages of free agency. But they enter another dimension this year. This was the first time they had salary cap problems severe enough to force them to get rid of players in order to field a full roster — Pegram and Miller. It promises only to get more difficult as they try to lock up some of their All-Pros, like center Dermontti Dawson.

They also have been lucky enough, in an odd way, not to have a great quarterback who would command $8 million annually. If Stewart continues the pace he set this summer over the next two years, he will become that, and then what do they do? And if he fails at quarterback, what then?

The Steelers have done well on the field and off since 1992. This year they should find out whether it is reasonable that they can continue doing so. ✦

Norm Johnson leaps into the arms of holder Mike Tomczak after kicking a field goal to defeat the Patriots in overtime.

1997 Game Of The Year:
Grand Theft
A torrent of turnovers sinks the Ravens and keeps the Steelers atop the AFC Central

By Ed Bouchette, Post-Gazette Sports Writer

Vinny Testaverde had the flu and the Steelers spent the night shouting, ``Bless you! Bless you! Bless you!"

Testaverde, an old friend of the Steelers, threw interceptions on his first three series to help them get well and run off to a 37-0 victory last night in Three Rivers Stadium.

It kept the Steelers tied for first with Jacksonville at 7-3 in the AFC Central Division and virtually knocked the Ravens out of contention at 4-6. It was the Steelers' sixth win in the past seven games, their only loss coming in Kansas City last Monday.

Jerome Bettis ran for 114 yards, his seventh 100-yard game of the season, and Yancey Thigpen caught six passes for 130 yards, his fourth over 100.

The Steelers jumped in front 20-0 at halftime through no remarkable effort from their offense.

The Ravens lost six turnovers in the first half — four interceptions and two fumbles. The Steelers scored four times off of them — 1-yard TD runs by Bettis and Kordell Stewart, and field goals of 52 and 22 yards by Norm Johnson.

Johnson kicked a field goal from 39 yards to open the scoring in the second half, swelling the Steelers' lead to 23-0. Stewart threw a 52-yard touchdown pass to Thigpen in the third quarter for a 30-0 lead. Rookie George Jones scored his first rushing touchdown, from the 1 in the fourth quarter to make it 37-0.

It was the first shutout in the storied two-year history of the Baltimore Ravens.

They made it look easy last night, intercepting three of Testaverde's passes. He had taken intravenous fluids Saturday night for the flu.

Stewart hooked up with Thigpen for three completions of 16, 11 and 9 yards as they moved to the Ravens' 24. Johnson kicked a 42-yard field goal that was good but negated by Mark Bruener's holding penalty.

The kick was so strong that Coach Bill Cowher allowed him to kick it from 52 and it was good again for a 10-0 Steelers lead with 2:24 left in the first quarter.

Carnell Lake, who moved back to strong safety for this game, made it three Testaverde drives, three Testaverde interceptions when the Ravens quarterback delivered a deep one just as he was getting hit by linebacker Greg Lloyd.

The Steelers did not convert that turnover, but Baltimore Coach Ted Marchibroda had seen enough. He replaced Testaverde with backup Eric Zeier. Someone must have forgotten to tell Steelers safety Darren Perry, who has five career inteceptions against Testaverde.

He made Zeier his victim this time on the quarterback's first pass. It hit Eric Green in the wrong place - the belly - as Lake crashed into him. The ball popped up and Perry snagged it on the run, returning it 42 yards to the 1.

Stewart jumped over the line on a quarterback sneak for his eighth rushing touchdown, which is tied for third most in NFL history. The score gave the Steelers a 17-0 lead with 13:22 left in the first half. ✦

Matt Freed

Cowher Power

REGULAR SEASON (11-5)

Date	Visitor		Home	
8/31/97	Cowboys	37	Steelers	7
9/7/97	Redskins	13	Steelers	14
9/22/97	Steelers	21	Jaguars	30
9/28/97	Oilers	24	Steelers	37
10/5/97	Steelers	42	Ravens	34
10/12/97	Colts	22	Steelers	24
10/19/97	Steelers	26	Bengals	10
10/26/97	Jaguars	17	Steelers	23*

Date	Visitor		Home	
11/3/97	Steelers	10	Chiefs	13
11/9/97	Ravens	0	Steelers	37
11/16/97	Bengals	3	Steelers	20
11/23/97	Steelers	20	Eagles	23
11/30/97	Steelers	26	Cardinals	20*
12/7/97	Broncos	24	Steelers	35
12/13/97	Steelers	24	Patriots	21*
12/21/97	Steelers	6	Oilers	16

PLAYOFFS

*OT

Date	Visitor		Home	
1/3/98	Patriots	6	Steelers	7
1/11/98	Broncos	24	Steelers	21

INDIVIDUAL STATS

PASSING

Name	CMP	ATT	PCT	YDs	YPC	TDs	INTs	Sacks	Rating
Stewart	236	440	53.6	3020	6.9	21	17	0	75.2
Tomczak	16	24	66.7	185	7.7	1	2	0	68.9
Quinn	1	2	50	10	5	0	0	0	64.6

KICKING

Name	XP	XPA	FG	FGA	Points
Johnson	40	40	22	25	106

PUNTING

Name	att	avg	Inside 20
Miller	64	42.6	0

RUSHING

Name	ATT	YDS	AVG	TDs
Bettis	375	1665	0	7
Stewart	88	476	1	11
Jones	72	235	0	1
McAfee	13	41	0	0
Hawkins	5	17	0	0
Blackwell	2	14	1	0
Tomczak	7	13	0	0
Witman	5	11	0	0
Lester	2	9	0	0
Thigpen	1	3	0	0
Marsh	1	2	0	0
Miller	1	-7	-1	0

RECEIVING

Name	REC	YDS	AVG	TDs
Thigpen	79	1398	17.7	7
Johnson	46	568	12.3	2
Hawkins	45	555	12.3	3
Blackwell	12	168	14	1
Bruener	18	117	6.5	6
Bettis	15	110	7.3	2
Jones	16	96	6	1
Lester	10	51	5.1	0
McAfee	2	44	22	0
Adams	1	39	39	0
Lyons	4	29	7.3	0
Marsh	2	14	7	0
Sadowski	1	12	12	0
Botkin	1	11	11	0
Witman	1	3	3	0

INTERCEPTIONS

Name	INT
Woolford	4
Perry	4
Lake	3
Scott	2
Oldham	2
Kirkland	2
Henry	1
Conley	1
Bell	1

SACKS

Name	Sacks
Lake	6
Kirkland	5
Gildon	5
Oldham	4
Lloyd	4
Holmes	4
Henry	4
Conley	4
Vrabel	2
Bell	2
Roye	1
Perry	1
Fuller	1

1998

Window Of Opportunity

Steelers know their time could be running out

By Ed Bouchette, Post-Gazette Sports Writer

The Bulls have been running here for six years now, riding higher and higher, snapping records, building fortunes. Optimism is high. The future looks good.

Can this run of wealth never end? Or does a Bear market lurk, the inevitable downward swing on the horizon?

Is time running out on the Steelers' chances to win a Super Bowl?

They have been on the second-best run in their history, topped only by those four Super Bowl winners of the 1970s. They have made the playoffs the past six years, won five division championships, reached three AFC title games and one Super Bowl.

But they haven't won the big one yet, and as they prepare to take another shot at it, questions again follow them as to how long this window of opportunity will remain open in a professional sport's system designed to penalize and erode success.

"I think a lot of it goes in cycles," linebacker Levon Kirkland admitted. "So, yeah, it's that time. You get sick and tired of coming close. Maybe we can do it this year. I think we're making strides doing that. I don't know what the future holds, but right now our expectations are to go to the Big Dance."

They flirted again with that date last January but came up short for the second time in an AFC championship at home, losing to Denver by three points.

Then the Broncos won the Super Bowl, allowing the

Steelers to wonder what might have been.

"Shoulda, coulda, woulda," center Dermontti Dawson said. "I wish it would have been us but I'm happy for those guys."

The "if" word has followed the Steelers for six years now. Cowher joined them in 1992 and has a chance to do something no other coach has done in the history of the NFL — take a team to the playoffs in each of his first seven years. It has been a good run, made despite more than 30 player defections to free agency. There have been disappointments in the playoffs because they have come so close to making it more than a good run. They lost twice at home in the AFC championship by four points to San Diego and three to Denver, and they had the ball in the fourth quarter against Dallas in the Super Bowl, trailing by just three points when Neil O'Donnell threw his second interception to Larry Brown.

Success in the NFL is difficult to maintain because the league makes the schedule tougher and the draft position worse for the good teams. Free agency and the salary cap have added to the woes of the good. The Steelers, so far, have thrived in this era, but there is a theory that it cannot last.

Even without free agency, the great team of the 1970s had a run of about eight seasons, from 1972 through 1979, and then it was over.

"The opportunities have been there," said Dawson. "We just didn't capitalize on them. Sooner or later,

Cowher Power

Peter Diana

Tampa Bay Buccaneers defensive tackle Warren Sapp closes in on Kordell Stewart as the Steelers' QB passes in the first quarter of the Hall of Fame Game in Canton, Ohio.

Andy Starnes

you never know what's going to happen because the years keep going by and guys are going to keep leaving. You're not going to have the same corps of guys here. It's always tough when you lose some of your better players. Each year we seem to lose one or two. It's hard to rebound from that." Carnell Lake, an All-Pro strong safety moved to cornerback to make up for some of those losses, said this summer that the Steelers could have gone to two or three Super Bowls during this run if they had just kept one or two free agents who got away, including Rod Woodson.

But the core of this team really isn't that old and it has thrived despite the losses of such talent as Woodson, Greg Lloyd, Chad Brown, Kevin Greene, Neil O'Donnell, Hardy Nickerson, Willie Williams, Ernie Mills and many other starters.

Among the core of stars now, Dawson is 33, Lake 31,

Kordell Stewart runs with the ball as the Steelers defeat the Chicago Bears 17-12 at Three Rivers Stadium.

Will Wolford 34, Justin Strzelczyk 30. Every other key starter is under 30. Kirkland is 29, Earl Holmes 25, Jerome Bettis 26, Kordell Stewart 25, Joel Steed 29.

"You have to take one year at a time and try to seize the moment," Cowher said. "I look at our football team and I don't see a true window. I think we have a good, solid football team. We have a young quarterback. We have a solid offensive line and some guys who have played for us for a while. We don't have many players left on this football team from that Super Bowl team because of free agency. Yet here we are two years later and we were three points from going to the Super Bowl again

Peter Diana

Jerome Bettis sprints through a huge hole in the center of the Carolina Panthers defense.

Andy Starnes

Carnell Lake returns an interception against the Bears.

with a lot of different faces.

"The important thing is to try to keep a good nucleus and not have a lot of change at once. Change is inevitable in this business, but you don't want to have wholesale change. I think we've been able to avoid that pretty good to this point."

It can even be argued that such change has helped the Steelers, that free agency has been more of an aid to them than a hindrance because they have done so well judging talent — which of their own players to keep, which to let go, which free agents to sign and which college players to draft.

In contrast, the Super Bowl teams of the 1970s stayed together, won together and grew old together. The teams of the 1990s, of course, have not come close to matching the heights of the 1970s, but perhaps the player movement will help them keep their run going.

Defensive end Nolan Harrison joined the Steelers

last year after spending six seasons with the Oakland Raiders and thinks they are smart enough as an organization to be able to continue to thrive.

"They've proven no matter how many people they lose, they have the minds upstairs to bring in whatever people they need to fill those spots and win. It's been proven that this team has found a way to keep it going.

"I look at that Super Bowl picture and there's only 27 guys left from that team. Yet we almost made it last year. This team and this management has found a way to bring people in. They have a good eye for talent. They know what they want, and they know how to go out and get it."

Now it's time, again, for them to do that on the field. ✦

Cowher Power

Peter Diana

Jerome Bettis celebrates a touchdown against the Buffalo Bills in a pre-season game at Three Rivers Stadium.

1998 Game Of The Year:
Tails Of Woe
Steelers flipped out over bizarre loss to Lions

By Ed Bouchette, Post-Gazette Sports Writer

They make sure their eyes are sharp, but has anyone ever thought about putting NFL officials through a hearing test?

The crew of officials blew more than their share of calls on the field yesterday on both sides, but nothing in football history can equal the mistake that referee Phil Luckett made that led to the Detroit Lions' 19-16 victory over the Steelers in overtime.

Has any official ever called the coin toss wrong, at any level in which football has been played?

Norm Johnson's 25-yard field goal with one second left sent yesterday's game into overtime after the offensively sluggish Steelers had blown a 13-3 lead in the second half with the help of a botched kickoff return. Jerome Bettis and Carnell Lake came out for the coin toss to determine which team would get the chance to receive in the sudden-death overtime.

Luckett told Bettis to call it in the air. Bettis called "tails," and the CBS-TV audio caught him saying just that. The coin landed tails, but Luckett stunned both the Steelers and Lions when he awarded it to Detroit.

The Lions took the kickoff, moved to the Steelers' 24 with the help of another controversial call and Jason Hanson kicked a 42-yard field goal to win the game and drive Bill

Cowher bonkers.

The Steelers coach screamed at the officials as they marched into their locker room after the game, accusing them of deciding the game, according to a KDKA-TV producer at the scene.

"What makes me mad is when you fight and scratch for 60 minutes out there and it's decided by people who wear striped shirts," Cowher said afterward. "There's something wrong with that."

Bettis and Lake were dumbfounded by Luckett's call. The official said he heard Bettis say "heads-tails" as the coin was in the air, so he went with what was first called.

"It was a ridiculous call and we lose the game because of it," said Bettis, who said he called tails and nothing else. "I'm at a loss for words. I can't believe a referee with that experience would make a call like that."

Lake backed up Bettis. Even Detroit's Robert Porcher, representing the Lions for the coin toss, apparently could not believe it. Porcher would not say what happened, but laughed in the locker room about the call and said, "All I know is, we got the ball."

The Steelers' defense, of course, could have overcome the error by stopping the Lions, but they did not. Herman Moore, who burned Lake often in the second half, beat him over the middle to catch a 28-yard pass from quarterback Charlie Batch to the Steelers' 37. That put them in range of Hanson, who already had kicked a 51-yard field goal in the third quarter.

But the Steelers came up with what appeared to be a huge defensive play on third-and-11 at the 38. Chris Oldham and Darren Perry sacked Batch back to the 48 and out of field goal range.

Oldham, though, was called for a facemask penalty. The officials have a choice on those: They can rule it was blatant and award 15 yards or that it was unintentional and mark off 5. They gave him 15, which sent Cowher into orbit.

"How can you call 15 yards on a facemask where he never grabbed it?" Cowher said. "What kind of judgment call is that?"

The victory improved the Lions' record to 5-7 and dropped the Steelers' to 7-5. ✦

Andy Starnes

Cowher Power

REGULAR SEASON (7-9)

Date	Visitor		Home		Date	Visitor		Home	
9/6/98	Steelers	20	Ravens	13	11/9/98	Packers	20	Steelers	27
9/13/98	Bears	12	Steelers	17	11/15/98	Steelers	14	Oilers	23
9/20/98	Steelers	0	Dolphins	21	11/22/98	Jaguars	15	Steelers	30
9/27/98	Seahawks	10	Steelers	13	11/26/98	Steelers	16	Lions	19*
10/11/98	Steelers	20	Bengals	25	12/6/98	Patriots	23	Steelers	9
10/18/98	Ravens	6	Steelers	16	12/13/98	Steelers	3	Buccaneers	16
10/26/98	Steelers	20	Chiefs	13	12/20/98	Bengals	25	Steelers	24
11/1/98	Oilers	41	Steelers	31	12/28/98	Steelers	3	Jaguars	21

*OT

INDIVIDUAL STATS

PASSING

Name	CMP	ATT	PCT	YDs	YPC	TDs	INTs	Sacks	Rating
Stewart	252	458	55	2560	10.2	11	18	33	62.9
Tomczak	21	30	70	204	9.7	2	2	2	83.2
Ward	1	1	100	17	17	0	0	0	118.8

RUSHING

Name	ATT	YDS	AVG	TDs
Bettis	316	1185	0	3
Stewart	81	406	1	2
Huntley	55	242	0	1
McAfee	18	111	1	0
Hawkins	10	41	0	0
Fuamatu-ma'afala	7	30	0	2
Ward	1	13	1	0
Johnson	1	4	0	0
Witman	1	2	0	0

RECEIVING

Name	REC	YDS	AVG	TDs
Johnson	65	815	12.5	7
Hawkins	66	751	11.4	1
Blackwell	32	297	9.3	1
Ward	15	246	16.4	0
Bruener	19	157	8.3	2
Bettis	16	90	5.6	0
Dunn	9	87	9.7	0
Fuamatu-ma'afala	9	84	9.3	1
Witman	13	74	5.7	0
Coleman	4	49	12.3	1
Lester	9	46	5.1	0
McAfee	9	27	3	0
Lyons	3	19	6.3	0
Huntley	3	18	6	0
Stewart	1	17	17	0
Bishop	1	4	4	0

KICKING

Name	XP	XPA	FG	FGA	Points
George	2	2	0	1	2
Johnson	21	21	26	31	99

PUNTING

Name	att	avg	Inside 20
Miller	81	43.6	34
Stewart	1	35	0

INTERCEPTIONS

Name	INT
Washington	5
Lake	4
Perry	2
Emmons	1
Holmes	1
Kirkland	1
Flowers	1
Oldham	1

SACKS

Name	Sacks
Gildon	11
Emmons	4
Roye	4
Henry	4
Harrison	4
Jones	3
Vrabel	2
Holmes	2
Kirkland	2
Gibson	2
Lake	1
Steed	1
Flowers	1
Perry	0

1999

Ready Or Not

Steelers sputtering as the opener dawns

By Ed Bouchette, Post-Gazette Sports Writer

Hire a new coordinator, put in a new offense, change the receivers around, switch some linemen, give the quarterback a fat new contract and: Presto! Same story.

The Steelers' offense has changed, but so far nothing has changed. The team that could not score last season has done little of it this summer, and the word "inconsistency" pops up more in Bill Cowher's conversations than "touchdowns."

Cowher and coordinator Kevin Gilbride expected things to develop slowly as the offense was introduced and with it the intricate option routes the receivers must run.

But now they have the extra burden of opening the season Sunday night at Cleveland, where the pitch will be feverish, uncertain about the most consistent thing on their offense the past three years, running back Jerome Bettis.

Cowher expects Bettis to play, but he also expects him to be less than The Bus everyone's come to expect. He has not played a down in the preseason and practiced only last week after Aug. 2 surgery to repair his left knee.

Cowher listed Bettis as questionable for Sunday's game.

"I told Jerome this," Cowher said, "to me I don't care who you are, for anyone to think they can go through a preseason and training camp without

practicing and think they're going to be at the top of their game . . . it's not done.

"Certainly, you can't expect Jerome to come out without having preseason work and expect him to be at the top of his game. It's going to take him a couple of weeks, no question about it, and you'd be foolish to expect that not be the case."

And that being the case, backup running backs Richard Huntley and rookie Amos Zereoue will play even if Bettis is able to play. Cowher listed another backup, Chris Fuamatu-Ma'afala, as doubtful for Sunday with a high ankle sprain.

The coach believes it's more important to have Bettis healthy for most of the season than overuse him in the opener.

"Going into this game, the most important thing to recognize is we do have 16 weeks in the regular season, that he's going to carry a big bulk of the load. It's important to keep that in perspective, not to diminish the importance of this game. I think Richard Huntley and Amos Zereoue are going to play a lot in this game as well."

Huntley has averaged just 2.8 yards rushing on 24 carries, while Zereoue led the Steelers with 170 yards and had a 4.0 average.

The statistics nearly across the board on offense through four exhibition games were poor. They scored five touchdowns on offense. They averaged 251.5 yards per game, 35 yards lower than they

Peter Diana

Jerome Bettis would pound out more than 1,000 yards in a tough season for the Steelers.

Lake Fong

Troy Edwards returns a punt against the Jacksonville Jaguars at Three Rivers Stadium.

the new offense.

"There are things we're doing that repetition is the only answer for. It seems to be we're very close, but it seems like I keep saying the same thing — it's one guy here, one guy there. If we make a block on a screen pass the other night, it's going to go out the gate. If we catch a couple balls, it's first-and-10. Little things that just destroy the momentum that you have to gain in this business to get on a roll, particularly in your play-calling.

"We've missed a block here, dropped a pass here. We had a fumble the other day when we get across the 50 [by rookie Troy Edwards], it could have been a long gainer. A lot of couldas and wouldas, but they didn't happen."

Cowher has been happy with quarterback Kordell Stewart, who produced an 80.6 passer rating in the preseason and would have completed 7 of 8 passes in his brief play Saturday if tight ends Mark Bruener and Mitch Lyons had not each dropped one.

"He declined a lot of chances to go to a lot of places — the Quarterback Challenge and other things," Cowher said of Stewart's off-season work. "He stayed right here in this building with Kevin. He feels comfortable. I thought he threw the ball very well the other night. I think his mindset is very good; it's as good as it's ever been."

While his offense may not have knocked 'em dead in the preseason, Cowher sees better days ahead.

"You implement a system, then you have to expand and head into a direction that exploits some of the strengths you have on your team. That's what we're in the process of doing.

"We have a good foundation of football players. We just have to do things more consistently. We are very close to becoming a productive team, but we aren't doing it and we're not there yet." ✦

averaged in 1998, when they ranked 25th of 30 NFL teams.

They averaged 149 yards passing in the four games, 10.5 yards lower than their norm last year when their passing output was second lowest in the league.

"I don't think you can sit up here and say we've been pleased with the degree of execution we've had," Cowher said of his offense. "We're going to have to become a more consistent football team offensively than we have shown to this point."

Cowher had predicted it would take time with

Andy Starnes

Kordell Stewart watches the remaining seconds tick off the clock in a loss against the Jacksonville Jaguars.

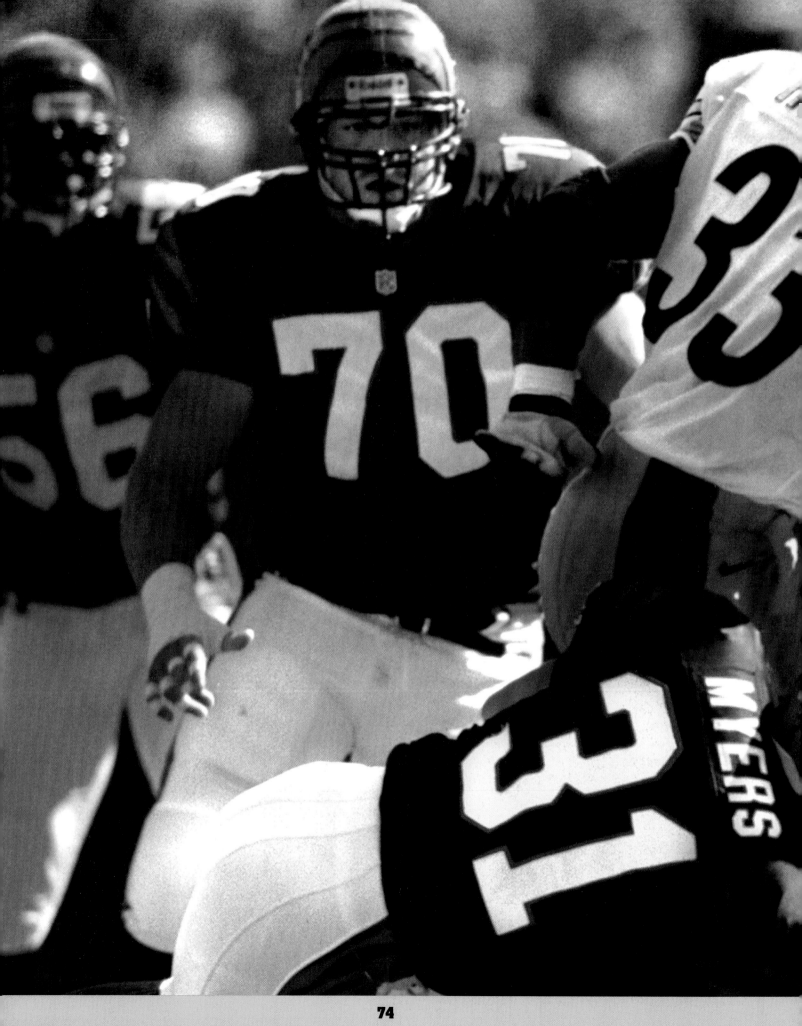

Richard Huntley runs for daylight during a game against the Bengals.

Peter Diana

1999 Game Of The Year:
"It's Embarrassing"
Steelers hit rock bottom with last-second loss to expansion Browns

By Ed Bouchette, Post-Gazette Sports Writer

That was some weekend the city just celebrated. They waved goodbye to Pitt Stadium Saturday, and yesterday they saluted the end of the Steelers' season.

The expansion Cleveland Browns lugged the worst defense in the NFL into Three Rivers Stadium yesterday and turned the Steelers season to rubble with a last-second, 16-15 victory that added another shade to the Steelers' color scheme: red.

"Yes, it's embarrassing," said linebacker Earl Holmes. "Not to take anything away from the Browns, but it's very embarrassing."

The Steelers' defense did take an interception and a fumble away from the Browns, the latter setting up their only touchdown. But they also gave up a quick, 80-yard touchdown drive to open the game and threw open the gate to allow the Browns to whip 58 yards in the final 1:51 with no timeouts left to set up rookie Phil Dawson's 39-yard field goal into the wind on the final play.

If it were the Jacksonville Jaguars or St. Louis Rams or one of the better teams in the league, it would have been bad. But the expansion Browns, who lost the opener to them, 43-0, and were two-touchdown underdogs in this one?

"It hurts for a team who has only won one game to come in our back yard and beat us," safety Lee Flowers said. "I definitely never imagined losing to Cleveland today." In Cleveland, they were "talking trash the whole day," Browns cornerback Corey Fuller said, "Here, they were quiet."

That about describes the Steelers' season today, too. Quiet. At 5-4, they technically remain in the thick of the playoff race. But all four losses have come to AFC teams, and the symbolism of losing at home to one of the NFL's worst teams was striking. They also lost cornerback Chad Scott for at least a few games with a sprained right knee.

"I'm not going to say it's the most embarrassing loss," linebacker Levon Kirkland said, "because you never know what's going to come up next."

That might be the scariest part, with games at Jacksonville, at Tennessee and at Kansas City. But the worst might be the ones at home, because they cannot win here. They are 1-3 at Three Rivers Stadium this season, 1-5 dating to the end of last season.

"Obviously," Flowers said, "We play better on the road. So we might need to put all our games on the road now."

Flowers predicted the Steelers have to win the rest of their games to make the playoffs. Yesterday, they looked more like a team capable of losing the rest of them than winning them all.

"We should have won this game today and we didn't," Flowers said, "and now we have to face the consequences this week."

And with seven games left, it could become their longest season in the eight-year tenure of Coach Bill Cowher.

"We gave up, pretty much," Flowers said. "We have to understand we take games one week at a time, we cannot underestimate guys. I think at some point we probably underestimated Cleveland a bit."

Or, maybe many are overestimating the Steelers, on offense and defense.

It was the Browns' first victory in Three Rivers Stadium since that epic, 51-0 blowout to open the 1989 season. But in many ways, this one was worse for the Steelers.

"Hopefully," Kirkland said, "we can turn this thing around and not panic in the moment, not drown ourselves in the moment."

First, they must find a pulse. ✦

Franka Bruns

REGULAR SEASON (6-10)

Date	Visitor		Home	
9/12/99	Steelers	43	Browns	0
9/19/99	Steelers	23	Ravens	20
9/26/99	Seahawks	29	Steelers	10
10/3/99	Jaguars	17	Steelers	3
10/10/99	Steelers	21	Bills	24
10/17/99	Steelers	17	Bengals	3
10/25/99	Falcons	9	Steelers	13
11/7/99	Steelers	27	49ers	6

Date	Visitor		Home	
11/14/99	Browns	16	Steelers	15
11/21/99	Steelers	10	Titans	16
11/28/99	Bengals	27	Steelers	20
12/2/99	Steelers	6	Jaguars	20
12/12/99	Ravens	31	Steelers	24
12/18/99	Steelers	19	Chiefs	35
12/26/99	Panthers	20	Steelers	30
1/2/2000	Titans	47	Steelers	36

*OT

INDIVIDUAL STATS

PASSING

Name	CMP	ATT	PCT	YDs	YPC	TDs	INTs	Sacks	Rating
Stewart	160	275	58.2	1464	5.3	6	10	22	64.9
Tomczak	139	258	53.9	1625	6.3	12	8	15	75.8
Bettis	1	1	100	21	21	1	0	0	158.3
Gonzalez	1	1	100	8	8	0	0	0	100

KICKING

Name	XP	XPA	FG	FGA	Points
Brown	30	31	25	29	105

PUNTING

Name	att	avg	Inside 20
Miller	84	45.2	27

RUSHING

Name	ATT	YDS	AVG	TDs
Bettis	299	1091	0	7
Huntley	93	567	1	5
Stewart	56	258	1	2
Zereoue	18	48	0	0
Tomczak	16	19	0	0
Witman	6	18	0	0
Fuamatu-ma'afala	1	4	0	0
Ward	2	-2	0	0
Gonzalez	2	-3	0	0
Miller	2	-9	0	0

RECEIVING

Name	REC	YDS	AVG	TDs
Edwards	61	714	11.7	5
Ward	61	638	10.5	7
Shaw	28	387	13.8	3
Hawkins	30	285	9.5	0
Huntley	27	253	9.4	3
Blackwell	20	186	9.3	0
Bruener	18	176	9.8	0
Stewart	9	113	12.6	1
Bettis	21	110	5.2	0
Witman	12	106	8.8	0
Lyons	8	81	10.1	0
Cushing	2	29	14.5	0
Johnson	2	23	11.5	0
Zereoue	2	17	8.5	0

INTERCEPTIONS

Name	INT
Shields	4
Washington	4
Davis	1
Emmons	1
Kirkland	1
Roye	1
Scott	1
Oldham	1

SACKS

Name	Sacks
Gildon	8
Emmons	6
Flowers	5
Roye	4
Steed	3
Oldham	3
Vrabel	2
Porter	2
Kirkland	2
Shields	1
Henry	1

2000

Seat Of Power

After two losing seasons and a tumultuous off-season, all eyes are on Cowher

By Ed Bouchette, Post-Gazette Sports Writer

The new executive-style chair in Bill Cowher's new office in the Steelers' new facility on the South Side has leather upholstery. It is black, not the fiery red or orange that might be more suitable for depicting the one Cowher occupies: A hot seat. He is, after all, the coach of the Steelers, who have gone 7-9 and 6-10 under his watch the past two seasons and have won only six of their past 21 games. He kept his job this year after the Steelers tumbled to seven losses in their final eight games of 1999 — including those to expansion Cleveland and dreadful Cincinnati at home. He kept it after he banished the starting quarterback to receiver for the final third of the season. After he offered to resign.

His resignation wasn't accepted and Tom Donahoe was ejected as director of football operations in a surprise move because of a growing conflict between Donahoe and Cowher.

So, the assumption is that Cowher sits on a hot seat, that if the Steelers continue on their losing path, the coach will follow Donahoe out the door. The Steelers have not had three straight losing seasons since Chuck Noll's first three, 1969-71.

Indeed, in a CNN/SI poll conducted over the weekend that asked which NFL coach was on the hottest of hot seats, Cowher came in second with 20 percent of the vote. Washington's Norv Turner fin-

ished first with 63 percent.

But Cowher is not a man acting as though his bottom is warm from sitting on his new seat, nor do his employers talk as if the heat is on. Cowher seems to be in his best mood since he took over as coach in 1992.

Maybe being on the hot seat has warmed him to the task.

"I don't worry about that," Cowher said, sitting comfortably in his leather chair. "I don't even concern myself with it. I don't think about it. I approach this as it's an important year to re-establish this football team and I'm very determined to do that.

"Where my future takes me is not in my hands. I'm doing everything I can. I will continue to do that as long as I'm here. I hope I'm here a long time.

"I don't want to just have a job. Don't concern myself with just wanting to have a job. I want to have the best team in the National Football League, to win a championship. That's what motivates me. That's the thing I look to do every year I step into this. I don't even look at it any other way than that. That's how you should approach any responsibility you have."

Cowher enters his ninth season as the Steelers' head coach, tied with Minnesota's Dennis Green for the longest active career with one NFL team. In the

Peter Diana

Chris Fuamatu-Ma'afala picks up 23 yards against the Jaguars in Jacksonville.

Peter Diana

Kent Graham is stopped and prevented from getting up by Courtney Brown as the Browns run out the clock in Cleveland.

four major professional sports, Cowher and Green are fourth in longevity with one team.

The Steelers coach has three years left on his contract at an estimated $2 million a season. The money is guaranteed, although Cowher offered to let the club out of the deal if they accepted his resignation last January.

"We had talks," Cowher said. "I'd rather not go into any specifics about it. The bottom line, again, is whatever's in the best interests of the Pittsburgh Steelers is what I wanted the decision to be made for. I did not want to be head coach of this football team than for any other reason than I was the right guy. As long as Mr. Rooney felt that way, I was glad to be allowed to stay.

"I like this job. I've been very blessed."

Dan Rooney and his son Art chose not to accept their coach's resignation and instead asked for Donahoe's. They hired Kevin Colbert to replace him.

Dan Rooney insists the coach is under no more scrutiny than any Steelers coach in any season.

"He's not any different than he ever was," Rooney said. "First of all, look, we're in the business that you have to win. That's the same every year. This is no different than any other year. A lot of people try to say we've done poorly the past two years, therefore ...

"By no means am I saying that this is some defining year and that if we don't have some certain win-lose record, that's it. I've always said you can have a winning season and it's a bad situation; you can have a losing season and it's a good situation. It's how you do it, what's happening.

"Obviously, you'll be asking me this as we go on and I'm going to give you the answer. We're going to look at this at the end of the year as we always

Cowher Power

Peter Diana

do. We're going to try to evaluate everything and everybody, say what happened and try to improve next year. That's what I think we did this year. We made some changes, some of which were perceived not that good or were not that accepted. I think we did the right thing and I think we have it in the right direction."

Rooney, then, does not have some ideal won-lost record that Cowher has to achieve in order to get a favorable job review — or to keep it.

"I think that the idea that he has to win, that we have to do this. . . ." Rooney said, pausing. "We have to look at the situation and say where we are, the development of the players. I mean these kids that are coming in. A guy like [Plaxico] Burress, I mean how's he going to do? He's not going to step in and be a world-beater right away. Hey, that is one position you can come in and make an impact;

Jerome Bettis tries to spin away from Baltimore Ravens linebacker Jamie Sharper during a season-opening shutout loss at Three Rivers Stadium.

you're still going to be better. I think [Troy] Edwards is going to be better than he was last year. That remains to be seen, there again."

Few expect much from the Steelers this season, yet Cowher has been more upbeat and has been more pleasant this year. He has been more open with the news media in many ways, including the information he provides about his team. Rooney has taken notice, and offered an opinion as to why.

"I don't want to get to talking about the Donahoe situation. I'd just as soon not. But there obviously was a strained relationship there. I had no problem with [Donahoe]. He said that and I said that, when all this was going on. But there was that strained relationship, which does not exist now, and I think that has a lot to do with being a positive. I think he also likes what he sees as far as the team, thinks that they have possibilities."

Cowher would not talk about his relationship with Donahoe and what transpired in January, and Donahoe declined to be interviewed for this story.

Colbert, who grew up on the North Side, came here from the Detroit Lions, where he was their pro personnel director. Colbert also was a scout under Coach Don Shula in Miami and worked with two coaches in Detroit — Wayne Fontes and Bobby Ross. He had heard stories that Cowher was difficult to work with.

"My response to that is I've been with Coach Shula," Colbert said. "Those guys who are really good, they're good for a reason. Sure, they're going to be gruff. There are going to be times when they're hard to work with. But that's why they are what they are, because they are so demanding.

"Yet, you have to understand the position that a head coach in this league is in. There's a lot of vast responsibilities when you really think about the things they are responsible for. So I can understand their being demanding. There was nobody more demanding than Don Shula.

"To me, what's the big deal? You hear different things but until you work with somebody, how are you going to know?"

Cowher and Colbert say they have worked well together, and Cowher admits that he has taken a new approach this season that, perhaps, he should have taken earlier when his playoff teams began losing veterans to free agency and the roster turned younger. He has a renewed passion, but he says it does not mean he lost his passion over the past few years.

"I don't know if I lost it. I really don't feel like I did. I look at two years ago and we're 6-2 and things are going one way and then we lose some close games and the next thing you know, you're in the middle of a tailspin.

"Last year, again, we had a pretty good start ... and lose a game we should have won [to Cleveland] ... Who knows what happens? And then we lose that. And for the first time last year had to deal with some of the outside issues."

Cowher became the second coach to break into the NFL with six straight playoff seasons, tying Paul Brown. His overall record of 77-51 is nearly identical to that of Noll, whose teams were 76-51-1 after 128 games. But then, Noll's teams had already won two Super Bowls by then.

"Losing's been a first," Cowher said. "These last couple of years have been foreign to me. So if it's done anything, I've found out about myself and you find out about the people you're surrounded with.

"You look within when the season's over to see what you need to do to change. You make changes to create a different approach and I think we've done that. I've tried to look within.

"Maybe you assume some things after you win and you've been in one place. You assume people recognize how you need to practice. You still have to re-establish that. You have to look at your team and see where your team is at.

"And if anything may have happened, this team as it became younger, I'm not so sure I changed my approach, which I think you have to do. If anything may have happened, that may have happened through the course of the last few years."

Cowher's not sure what to expect from this year's team.

"It's a young team and I know I've said that before. But it is. Consequently, it's hard to get a barometer on where you're at. That's probably why it's important that I am more open, it's important they understand what my expectations are as a coach. Whereas maybe in the past when you have a veteran team you don't necessarily send messages through your veteran players. Here, the young players have to become veterans quicker than maybe they're willing to accept it."

During training camp, Cowher often took a break in the middle of practice to gather the team around him. He was more vocal on the field.

"It was probably making sure that we didn't deviate from an approach that we had to establish. We talked about wanting to re-establish being a physical football team, being an up-tempo football team. Those are things you talk about, those are things you see happen on the first day. But all of a sudden you can fall quickly back into, you know, the easy way. It was more an attempt to make sure that they always understood that the foundation was going to be us fighting through that.

"It was to establish that it was going to be our basis. It's not something you turn on and off. We only know how to play disciplined, we only know how to play smart, because that's the way we practice. Because I firmly believe you play the way you practice.

"I believe with a young team that's going to happen. If we can establish good habits, which is what training camp does, it gives you a chance to maybe overcome any deficiences you have by becoming a smart, disciplined, tough football team and that's what we tried to do in camp."

Camp is over and so are the exhibition games. The real stuff begins Sunday. And when Cowher leads his team onto the field for the first game of their last season in Three Rivers Stadium, many will wonder if it will be his last here.

Peter Diana

Bill Cowher is congratulated by Levon Kirkland after beating the Oakland Raiders.

"I don't worry about that. I believe in the things I talk about, I really do. Look at my career. I've been a guy who has been counted out in everything I've ever done. I kind of like that, I thrive on that.

"There's a lot of exciting things happening with this football team, this new facility, a kind of new approach we've taken, and it's created a lot of excitement. And probably from my perspective, it's created an energy for me that I'm looking forward to it, the challenge of it, and I'm ready to deal with it head-on. Anything that comes." ✦

2000 Game Of The Year:

Flashback

Stewart rekindles memories of '97 with rout of Bengals

By Ed Bouchette, Post-Gazette Sports Writer

For one game, it was 1997 again. Same quarterback, same number, same kind of performance. It was as if someone else had pulled on the No. 10 jersey the past two years and did a poor imitation of Slash.

But yesterday, Kordell Stewart was a perfect 10.

On a day in which the Steelers could not stop the run, Stewart supplied the sizzle that had been missing since '97. He threw three touchdown passes and ran for another as the Steelers wore down the Cincinnati Bengals, 48-28.

"Kordell threw the ball very well," Coach Bill Cowher said. "He made some very good decisions, pulled the ball down at times. I don't think there's any question it was Kordell's best game of the season."

His three touchdown passes were half of his '99 total and just one short of the four he had coming into the game. They tied a personal best he accomplished twice in '97, his first season as a starting quarterback and his best, one that helped land them in the AFC championship game.

Stewart completed only 11 of 20 passes for 182 yards, but several incompletions should have been caught. He did not throw an interception, ran six times for 31 yards and averaged 16.5 yards a completion. He crisply guided an offense that included 185 yards rushing, 93 of those by Jerome Bettis.

"He looked like the Kordell of old," Bengals defensive end

Matt Freed

Michael Bankston said, "sitting back, hitting his receivers or, if all else fails, taking off through a seam and running for big yardage. He has a lot of talent."

This time a year ago, Cowher had banished him to wide receiver.

"I'm throwing touchdowns, running for some, handing the ball to Jerome," Stewart said. "That's what I love to do."

It was a good time for him to do it, too, because the Steelers' defense folded at the beginning instead of the end.

Corey Dillon ran for 128 of the Bengals' 209 yards against the Steelers one week after Fred Taylor gouged them for 234.

"Our run defense is one thing we have to get rectified," Cowher said.

The teams traded touchdowns early and often before the Steelers' defense finally found its composure long enough to help put away their sixth victory in 12 games and end a three-game losing streak. Cincinnati fell to 2-10.

"We weren't worrying about them scoring," said Hines Ward, who led the Steelers with four receptions for 70 yards and a touchdown. "We kept driving the ball up and down the field. That's real big when they come out and score and we come right back and score. That hurts them."

Bettis failed to get his sixth 100-yard game, but he scored a touchdown and pushed his season total to 1,019 yards, his fifth in a row with more than 1,000.

"It's hard to find any fault in anything we did offensively," Cowher said.

Stewart struck early when he found Ward on a slant down the middle on the game's sixth play for a 34-yard touchdown pass.

It was the opening shot of a volley of early scores. Brandon Bennett tied it when he ran 37 yards untouched around right end on the Bengals' first drive.

"For a long time, we haven't been on the same page," Bettis said of what had been the NFL's 24th-ranked offense. "It's good to see when we're on the same page what we can do."

It was chapter and page brought to them by Stewart.

"Kordell is capable of great things," Bruener said. "He just needs to be patient and understand he can. He played extremely well today. I think you'll see some better things in the future." ✦

Cowher Power

REGULAR SEASON (9-7)

Date	Visitor		Home	
9/3/2000	Ravens	16	Steelers	0
9/17/2000	Steelers	20	Browns	23
9/24/2000	Titans	23	Steelers	20
10/1/2000	Steelers	24	Jaguars	13
10/8/2000	Steelers	20	Jets	3
10/15/2000	Bengals	0	Steelers	15
10/22/2000	Browns	0	Steelers	22
10/29/2000	Steelers	9	Ravens	6

Date	Visitor		Home	
11/5/2000	Steelers	7	Titans	9
11/12/2000	Eagles	26	Steelers	23*
11/19/2000	Jaguars	34	Steelers	24
11/26/2000	Steelers	48	Bengals	28
12/3/2000	Raiders	20	Steelers	21
12/10/2000	Steelers	10	Giants	30
12/16/2000	Redskins	3	Steelers	24
12/24/2000	Steelers	34	Chargers	21

*OT

INDIVIDUAL STATS

PASSING

Name	CMP	ATT	PCT	YDs	YPC	TDs	INTs	Sacks	Rating
Stewart	151	289	52.2	1860	12.3	11	8	30	73.6
Graham	66	148	44.6	878	13.3	1	1	13	63.4
Bettis	0	2	0	0	0	0	1	0	0

RUSHING

Name	ATT	YDS	AVG	TDs
Bettis	355	1341	0	8
Stewart	78	436	1	7
Huntley	46	215	1	3
Fuamatu-ma'afala	21	149	1	1
Ward	4	53	1	0
Kreider	2	24	1	0
Zereoue	6	14	0	0
Graham	8	7	0	0
Witman	3	5	0	0
Edwards	3	4	0	0
Miller	1	0	0	0

RECEIVING

Name	REC	YDS	AVG	TDs
Shaw	40	672	16.8	4
Ward	48	672	14	4
Burress	22	273	12.4	0
Hawkins	19	238	12.5	1
Edwards	18	215	11.9	0
Bruener	17	192	11.3	3
Fuamatu-ma'afala	11	107	9.7	0
Bettis	13	97	7.5	0
Huntley	10	91	9.1	0
Geason	3	66	22	0
Kreider	5	42	8.4	0
Witman	5	33	6.6	0
Blackwell	2	23	11.5	0
Cushing	4	17	4.3	0

KICKING

Name	XP	XPA	FG	FGA	Points
Brown	32	33	25	30	107

PUNTING

Name	att	avg	Inside 20
Miller	90	43.8	34

INTERCEPTIONS

Name	INT
Scott	5
Washington	5
Alexander	3
Codie	1
Kirkland	1
Porter	1
Flowers	1

SACKS

Name	Sacks
Gildon	13.5
Porter	10.5
Smith	4
Townsend	3.5
Alexander	1.5
Battles	1
Vrabel	1
Holmes	1
Flowers	1

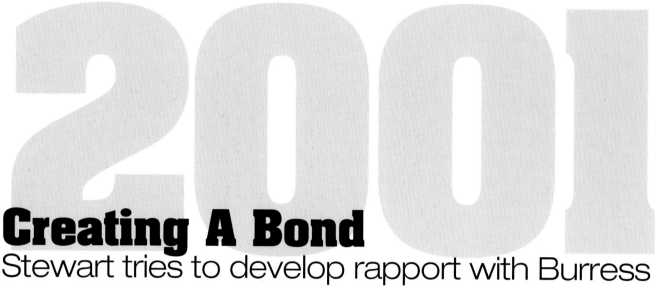

Creating A Bond
Stewart tries to develop rapport with Burress

By Gerry Dulac, Post-Gazette Sports Writer

A curious development took place Thursday night at Heinz Field, something not seen much in the Steelers' offense for nearly six years. For two series, or until Kordell Stewart was finished for the night, it appeared as if a quarterback and a wide receiver were trying to develop a special relationship.

Honest.

Three of Stewart's first four passes and seven of the 14 he attempted against the Buffalo Bills were directed at Plaxico Burress, the team's No. 1 draft pick last year who is trying to forget his disappointing rookie season.

Coach Bill Cowher tried to downplay the attention Burress was receiving, saying Stewart merely was going where the reads were taking him.

But offensive coordinator Mike Mularkey went a step farther, saying Stewart is starting to develop a trust that his second-year receiver will get open.

"That's nice to see," Mularkey said.

If the Steelers' passing game is going to improve, if it's going to move from the 29th spot it has occupied in the National Football League rankings two of the past three seasons, then it is up to Burress, the eighth overall pick in the 2000 draft, to produce numbers better than the 6-foot-6, 229-pound receiver posted last year.

And the only way that is going to happen is if he develops a bond with Stewart, who heads into the regular season as the unquestioned starter at quarterback.

The Steelers have not had a quarterback rely on a wide receiver so much since Yancey Thigpen caught a club-record 85 passes from Neil O'Donnell in 1995.

"The offense is built for everybody," Burress said. "You just can't say, I'm not going to get the ball on this play. In this offense, you can get the ball every play. That motivates me to work hard. If I go out and make plays, I think this offense will do well."

There was little evidence of Mularkey's offense during the preseason because the Steelers chose to keep wraps on their new attack, preferring to unveil it next Sunday in Jacksonville.

What it is designed to do, though, is put less responsibility on the receivers to read defensive coverages and allow them to run a lot of the same routes from different formations. The intent is to give Stewart a better idea of where his receivers are supposed to be and eventually develop the trust they are going to get open.

If the 20-0 victory against the Bills was any indication, Stewart will not be afraid to seek out his biggest target. And that could be a positive for a team that used back-to-back drafts to take a wide receiver on the first round, hoping to find a big-play performer to take some of the pressure off running back Jerome Bettis.

Matt Freed

Hines Ward eludes the Bills' Chris Watson after making a catch in Buffalo.

Matt Freed

"He worked hard this off-season and he has a lot to prove," said Hines Ward, the team's leading receiver the past two seasons. "He wants to go out and prove why the Steelers took him as a first round pick. That's what he's done this year. He has committed himself to getting better.

"Last year wasn't the year he wanted to have. He had to get back into working hard, what got him to be that first-round pick. A lot of players would get complacent being a first-round pick, thinking you can come out here and just dominate the game like you did in college. That's not necessarily true. Everyone in the pros is good. You just can't go out there and out-athlete somebody. It's all about technique and making plays. And he worked hard at camp, running routes, [working on] his hand-eye coordination. It's going to pay off for him."

That didn't happen last season. Burress had a good training camp and played well in preseason, but when the regular season started he was harder to

Kendrell Bell pulls down the Ravens' Obafemi Ayanbadejo.

find than Jimmy Hoffa. When he did surface, it was only because everyone noticed him dropping passes.

Burress said dropped passes in the Steelers' offense are magnified because the wide receivers don't get may chances to atone for their mistake.

"That's the worst thing you can do here is drop a football," Burress said. "You may get only two or three passes thrown at you [in a game]. If one gets batted down, you catch one and drop one, that's not a good day."

"I try to tell Plex, the opportunities we do get you have to capitalize on them," Ward said. "You can't take one drop and say, ' All right, I'll come back and catch the next one,' because there might not be a next one."

Burress finished the season with only 22 catches for 273 yards and no touchdowns. Worse, as the season

Matt Freed

Kordell Stewart is congratulated by Plaxico Burress after scoring a touchdown in the fourth quarter against the Jacksonville Jaguars at Heinz Field.

wore on, he stopped running routes when he knew he wasn't involved in the play. When he did that in Week 10 against the Philadelphia Eagles, he was benched and replaced in the starting lineup by Courtney Hawkins, a receiver who was on the roster only because of an injury to Will Blackwell.

Nothing went right. Even when the Steelers were faced for the first time with a situation that screamed for a fade pass to Burress, they ignored their rookie receiver and tried to throw a pass across the back of the end zone in Cleveland. That, and a wrong call by the officials, contributed to a 23-20 defeat.

Burress, though, has tried to change all that this season. He usually stayed after practice at training camp, working on his routes and doing drills designed to improve his catching ability.

"That's where there's a big change from last year," Ward said. "[Last year,] he might have a cover-two [defense] and jog on his route thinking he's not going to get it. But you get in there with Tommy [Maddox] — he threw a touchdown to Demetrius [Brown] in cover two [against the Detroit Lions] — you got to expect the ball on every play. And that's what he's done this year. He's worked hard on every route against every coverage. That's what helped him in the long run."

Perhaps that's why some trust appears to be developing between Burress and Stewart. Or maybe it was because Ward did not play against the Bills.

Plaxico Burress makes a catch over the Bengals' Rodney Heath.

Whatever the reason, the Steelers need Burress to become a dominant force in their lineup. He gets his chance now, with the regular season a week away, to prove he can handle the role.

"I just go out and play," Burress said. "If I can get the trust here and I'm catching balls like I know I can, the numbers will be there. I just want to be myself. I'm just going out and playing my style of football — just go out, relax, don't put pressure on myself when everybody is criticizing me. That's when the best of me comes out. That's when you're going to see what kind of player I am." ✦

Matt Freed

Amos Zereoue carries the ball in a game against the Bengals.

2001 Game Of The Year:
Special Defects
Touchdowns on blocked field goal, punt return stop Steelers' run to Super Bowl

By Ed Bouchette, Post-Gazette Sports Writer

Whether it's Dennis Gibson or Tony Martin or John Elway or someone named Antwan Harris. Three Rivers Stadium or Heinz Field. The names change, the teams change, everything changes except the results.

The AFC's No. 1 seed got planted, again. The New England Patriots, 10-point underdogs, ripped the AFC championship trophy from the Steelers' grasp in a story that has become all too familiar. It was the fourth championship game played on the North Side in the past eight seasons and the opponent danced away with a third victory.

The Patriots choked off the NFL's best running game, slammed their special teams and turned the Steelers' season upside down, pulling off a 24-17 victory to land in the Super Bowl in New Orleans Sunday against St. Louis. It was the seventh time in the past eight years the conference's No. 1 seed did not reach the Super Bowl.

"The vets told us you may never get chance to be in this position again, so you need to take advantage of it, and we didn't seize the moment today," said receiver Hines Ward.

The Steelers had more chances than any AFC team in history over an 8-year span other than their storied club from the 1970s, and they had their chances yesterday.

Many players were angry their special teams cost them 14 points when New England's Troy Brown returned a punt 55 yards for a touchdown to open the scoring and when Harris took a blocked field goal 49 yards for a touchdown in the third quarter to stake the Patriots to a 21-3 lead.

"The defense did not lose this game," safety Lee Flowers said. "The special teams lost this game, period. Given, we are a team, but the special teams lost the game, period."

Said Ward, "They killed us on special teams."

They had help. Kordell Stewart threw three interceptions, two at midfield in the final three minutes to snuff out drives that could have tied the score. He also lost a fumble in the third quarter when pulling guard Rich Tylski ran into him just after he took the snap.

Then there was the running game. The Patriots came out blitzing to stop the run and they did it like no other team. They held the Steelers to a season-low 58 yards rushing on 22 carries. Stewart had 34 on one run and led the team with 41 yards on eight carries. Jerome Bettis returned after six games to run nine times for 8 yards, tying his worst day as a Steeler.

It wasn't just special teams that cost the Steelers a shot at their second AFC championship in 22 years.

"I don't know if they were looking for the war we were ready to give them," said New England cornerback Ty Law, who grew up in Aliquippa and backed up some tough talk from early in the week. "We know how to play physical football and we came here to play that. I don't know why people don't seem to realize this. We proved that today. We outmuscled these guys."

The Steelers' defense, rated best in the NFL, held up its part. The Steelers held the Patriots to 67 yards rushing, and Flowers knocked out quarterback Tom Brady with a low hit in the second quarter.

But Drew Bledsoe, the former Pro Bowl quarterback who lost his job to Brady early in the season, came off the bench to throw an 11-yard touchdown to David Patten in the second quarter and complete some key passes on a fourth-quarter drive that ate up four precious minutes.

"They won; we feel we're the better team," said linebacker Joey Porter, who nearly intercepted a pass in the fourth quarter that might have changed the outcome. "But you can't say that when you lose. They won the game. All the best wishes to New England, I hope they win it."

"It's a horrible feeling," said special teams captain John Fiala, who played inside linebacker for the injured Earl Holmes. "We didn't perform today."

For the Steelers in AFC championship games at home, it's always something. ✦

Cowher Power

REGULAR SEASON (10-6)

Date	Visitor		Home		Date	Visitor		Home	
9/9/2001	Steelers	3	Jaguars	21	11/18/2001	Jaguars	7	Steelers	20
9/30/2001	Steelers	20	Bills	3	11/25/2001	Steelers	34	Titans	24
10/7/2001	Bengals	7	Steelers	16	12/2/2001	Vikings	16	Steelers	21
10/14/2001	Steelers	20	Chiefs	17	12/9/2001	Jets	7	Steelers	18
10/21/2001	Steelers	17	Buccaneers	10	12/16/2001	Steelers	26	Ravens	21
10/29/2001	Titans	7	Steelers	34	12/23/2001	Lions	14	Steelers	47
11/4/2001	Ravens	13	Steelers	10	12/30/2001	Steelers	23	Bengals	26*
11/11/2001	Steelers	15	Browns	12*	1/6/2002	Browns	7	Steelers	28

*OT

PLAYOFFS

Date	Visitor		Home	
1/20/2002	Ravens	10	Steelers	27
1/27/2002	Patriots	24	Steelers	17

INDIVIDUAL STATS

PASSING

Name	CMP	ATT	PCT	YDs	YPC	TDs	INTs	Sacks	Rating
Stewart	266	442	60.2	3109	11.7	14	11	29	81.7
Maddox	7	9	77.8	154	22	1	1	1	116.2
Bettis	1	2	50	32	32	1	0	0	135.4
Ward	0	1	0	0	0	0	0	1	39.6

KICKING

Name	XP	XPA	FG	FGA	Points
Brown	34	37	30	44	124

PUNTING

Name	att	avg	Inside 20
Miller	59	2505	23
Brown	3	106	0

RUSHING

Name	ATT	YDS	AVG	TDs
Bettis	225	1072	5	4
Stewart	96	537	6	5
Fuamatu-Ma'afala	120	453	4	3
Zereoue	85	441	5	1
Bowers	18	84	5	1
Ward	10	83	8	0
Kreider	7	29	4	1
Edwards	5	28	6	1
Witman	5	24	5	0
Maddox	6	9	2	1
Martin	1	8	8	0
Brown	1	6	6	0
Miller	1	0	0	0

RECEIVING

Name	REC	YDS	AVG	TDs
Burress	66	1008	15.3	6
Ward	94	1003	10.7	4
Shaw	24	409	17	2
Edwards	19	283	14.9	0
Zereoue	13	154	11.8	1
Fuamatu-Ma'afala	16	127	7.9	1
Bruener	12	98	8.2	0
Tuman	7	96	13.7	1
Bettis	8	48	6	0
Witman	6	32	5.3	0
Cushing	5	24	4.8	1
Blackwell	1	8	8	0
Kreider	2	5	2.5	0
Bowers	1	0	0	0

INTERCEPTIONS

Name	INT
Scott	5
Alexander	4
Logan	2
Townsend	2
Washington	1
Gildon	1
Hampton	1

SACKS

Name	Sacks
Gildon	12
Porter	9
Bell	9
Smith	8
Von Oelhoffen	4
Logan	2
Townsend	2
Alexander	2
Holmes	2
Bailey	2
Three with 1 sack	

2002

Steelers In Their Favorite Place
This team relishes super expectations

By Ed Bouchette, Post-Gazette Sports Writer

Expectations are up and the crowds are down at training camp. It's as if nothing counts for the Steelers until they get back to where they were at the end of the 2001 season, kicking off again for the AFC championship in Heinz Field.

Anything less may come as a disappointment to their fans, who had no reason to believe the Steelers would come within a touchdown of reaching the last Super Bowl and every reason to believe they will get to the next one.

The Steelers, after all, head into the 2002 season with no weaknesses, no holes, no serious injuries, no untested starters, no new coordinators, no excuses. They have the second-easiest schedule in the NFL, based on last year's won-lost records. They play in a new division where none of the other three members should be playoff contenders – or even finish with winning records.

That's what it says on paper, anyway. What was it that Lee Flowers called the Tampa Bay Buccaneers after the Steelers beat them last year? Oh, yes, "paper champions."

Those are the Steelers for 2002.

Now, just because all the odds-makers have the Steelers as the favorites in the AFC doesn't mean they can't fulfill the predictions. They were favored in 1979 and they went all the way, too.

It's not easy, which is why their greatest chance of winning one isn't this year, it was in January, when they were favored to whip the New England Patriots by 10 1/2 points. It wound up being a "special" game, all right. The Steelers outgained the Patriots, 306 yards to 259. Their offense outscored New England's, 17-10. Too bad they had to punt. Too bad they had to try a field goal from 34 yards. Put that chip-shot field goal by Kris Brown in the Steelers' register and they win, 20-17, even with the punt return they gave up for a touchdown.

But, enough about history. They say it's not often you get a second chance in life, but the Steelers are getting theirs.

Their team is nearly identical to the one that went 13-3, beat Baltimore in the playoffs and lost by a touchdown in the AFC championship to New England. They have a new inside linebacker, a new right guard, a new kicker, and that's it. They may have a better team than the one that compiled the second-best record in franchise history.

"You want to try to keep a good thing going," Coach Bill Cowher said.

All their good, young players – of which there are many – are a year older, a year wiser and, presumably, better because of it. Even someone such as Jeff Hartings should play better because he has one season behind him at center, a posi-

Cowher Power

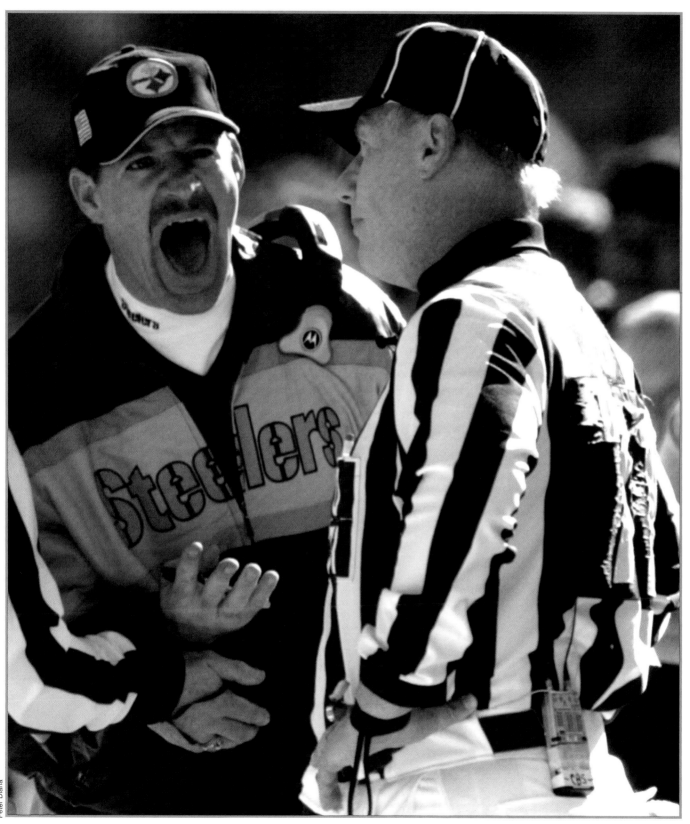

Bill Cowher disputes a first quarter New England touchdown with umpire Ed Coukart in the AFC championship game.

Gabor Degre

tion he never played before he arrived here last year. With the possible exception of halfback Jerome Bettis, all the starters should have their best years ahead.

They have all of their coaches back – except the one that took the fall for the special teams blowup against New England – and that should bode well for consistency on offense and defense. Their backup quarterback position was strengthened by the addition of Charlie Batch. Tommy Maddox has a year under his belt after he had not played in the NFL the previous five seasons.

As solid as Bobby Shaw was in the slot receiver position last season, rookie Antwaan Randle El should make more and bigger plays. No one expects their new kicker, Todd Peterson, to miss 14 field goals this season, not to mention five in a game.

They have the talent, they have the depth, they have the coaching, they have the schedule and they have the intangible chemistry of a championship team. All they have to do is go out and prove it, and that's the most difficult thing, especially in the NFL these days.

Brandon Mitchell blocks a Kris Brown field goal in the third quarter.

New England, their opening opponent, went from 5-11 to Super Bowl champions, making them the third straight to go from not having a winning season one year to champions the next. It's a phenomenon that's hard to explain and what it means is all the teams favored to win in those three seasons did not complete their missions.

"That's what you're trying to create," Cowher said. "In business, you're trying to create high expectations. That's not the pressure. The pressure, to me, is not being there."

The Steelers have spent more than $40 million in signing bonuses this year not only to keep the team together for one more season, but for several to come. They do not want to become the Baltimore Ravens – although they will take their Vince Lombardi trophy – and be forced to break up a winning team after a year or two. They went through that in the mid-90s.

"Obviously," Dan Rooney said, "we feel we have

Cowher Power

Peter Diana

BillCowher expresses himself to line judge Mark Steinkerchner and field judge Pete Morelli.

John Beale Photo

a good team that went pretty far last year... We feel we should give it another shot and give the fans a shot at it."

Complacency, however, can creep in. "You have to keep pushing yourself," Cowher said. "Complacency will start when you get a few players who don't think they have to be there. Our guys understand you have to work at it every year."

The Steelers had the No. 1 running game in the NFL in 2001, the No. 1 overall defense, the No. 1

defense against the rush, the No. 3 overall offense that may be better and more explosive with an improved passing game. Their kicking game should be better only because it can't get worse and the loss in the AFC title game got the message across like a 2-by-4 to the jaw. They hired a new coach for special teams and spent more time on them in training camp.

The Steelers jigsaw puzzle is in place. Now they must make sure the pieces don't get scattered. ✦

2002 Game Of The Year:
Heinz Catch-up
Fuamata-Ma'afala's touchdown run caps Steelers' stunning wild-card rally

By Ed Bouchette, Post-Gazette Sports Writer

Fans streamed out of Heinz Field like cheap, runny ketchup and boos cascaded from those who remained as the Steelers' defense gave up yet another touchdown, five minutes into the fourth quarter yesterday.

The Cleveland Browns, of all opponents, took a 12-point lead and were about to heap more playoff disappointment on the Steelers in their home.

"There were times," Steelers linebacker Joey Porter said, "you had to think in the back of your mind, here we go again."

But in less than five minutes, the Steelers turned what would have been another devastating playoff loss into one of their most memorable playoff victories when they rallied for two touchdowns in the closing minutes to defeat the Browns, 36-33.

"This," tackle Wayne Gandy said, "is the kind of game that propels you somewhere. Our guys decided they weren't going home today."

Chris Fuamatu-Ma'afala's 3-yard touchdown run with 54 seconds remaining in the game propelled the Steelers to a playoff game against the second-seeded Tennessee Titans.

Many called it the game of their lives.

"I don't think anybody in here's been part of a game where it ended like this," said Hines Ward, who caught a 5-yard touchdown pass from Tommy Maddox with 3:06 left to give the Steelers a chance. "I can't even describe the feeling right now. I've never in my whole life been part of a game like this."

Dan Rooney, who has seen a lot more games than Ward, ranked it second among exciting Steelers playoff games only to the Immaculate Reception victory against Oakland in 1972.

"This was a tremendous game," Rooney said.

The Cleveland Browns, who were 7 1/2-point underdogs, might disagree.

"I don't know that I've been as disappointed in a ballgame in an awful long time," Cleveland Coach Butch Davis said.

The Browns had a 33-21 lead late into the fourth quarter as backup quarterback Kelly Holcomb threw for 429 yards and three touchdowns.

Despite Maddox touchdown passes of 6 yards to Plaxico Burress late in the third quarter and 3 yards to Jerame Tuman in the fourth to cut the Browns' lead to 27-21, Cleveland increased its lead to 12 points when Andre Davis caught a 2-yard pass from Holcomb with 10:17 left in the game.

When the next Steelers series went nowhere, many fans had seen enough. But the real drama was about to unfold.

The Steelers started another series with 5:30 left and, with Maddox running the no-huddle offense and the Browns contributing three penalties, they moved 77 yards on 10 plays in 2 1/2 minutes to make the score 33-28 on the touchdown pass to Ward.

"The guys kept believing," Porter said. "We never stopped fighting, never stopped fighting. The defense knew if we gave the ball back to the offense one more time, they'd get it done."

William Green, who rushed for 178 yards last week against Atlanta, gained 3 yards on first down. Holcomb threw incomplete on second down and a delay-of-game penalty made it third-and-12 for the Browns from their 21. Holcomb put the ball right in the hands of Dennis Northcutt for a first down, but Northcutt dropped it.

Cleveland punted and, with 2:38 left, the Steelers began their winning drive on their 39 with 2:38 remaining.

Maddox – 30 of 48 for a team playoff record 367 yards, three touchdowns and two interceptions – completed 4 of 5 passes, starting with one of 24 yards to Burress. After an incompletion, he completed passes of 10 to Ward, 17 to Burress and 7 more to Ward down to the Browns' 3.

No one was leaving or booing in Heinz Field at that point, but everyone on it was sucking wind.

"I was exhausted," Burress said. "I was down on two knees. Hines was down on two knees. We ran the two-minute offense for the whole second half. The coaches weren't calling plays. Tommy was making his own calls."

A coach would call the next play, after taking their final timeout with 58 seconds left. Dick Hoak, a Steelers assistant since the Immaculate Reception year, suggested it: 42 Base, a handoff on the right side to Fuamatu-Ma'afala.

"We ran it earlier in the game," offensive coordinator Mike Mularkey said. "Got stuffed, got booed for it. Same play. We got down there and scored earlier to Hines. Same people, same formation, same look."

Same end result from the four-wide receiver formation when Fuamatu-Ma'afala ran to the right and bounced left into a hole for a touchdown on his second carry of the game. Antwaan Randle El threw a 2-point conversion pass to Tuman for a three-point lead.

The Browns tried desperately to get into field-goal range in the final 54 seconds, but time ran out after Holcomb's pass to Andre King at the Steelers' 29.

The Browns were bitter.

"I'll tell you this, they'll be home next week," Cleveland cornerback Corey Fuller said. "They got one more week. We gave it to them today. Unbelievable."

It was all of that.

Only Doug Williams, with 430 yards passing in 1988 for Washington, threw for more against the Steelers in any game.

The Browns opened in the no-huddle and scored quickly. Holcomb hit Kevin Johnson, who beat Hank Poteat for an 83-yard reception to the 1. Green scored on the next play for a 7-0 Cleveland lead.

The Steelers were driving at Cleveland's 23 when Maddox threw the first of his two interceptions to cornerback Daylon McCutcheon at the 3. Then Randle El muffed a punt that Cleveland recovered at the Steelers' 32. On the next play, Holcomb found Northcutt, who beat Poteat in the right corner of the end zone for a 14-0 Cleveland lead.

McCutcheon then picked off Maddox again, this time on a pass tipped at the line of scrimmage. But this time bad things happened for Cleveland on a punt.

Randle El returned a punt 66 yards for a touchdown that breathed some life into the Steelers, 14-7.

"No one felt worse than he did," Coach Bill Cowher said of Randle El's early drop. "The guy is a playmaker. I can't say enough about him."

The Steelers, though, slipped behind, 17-7, at the half after Phil Dawson's 31-yard field goal and Jeff Reed's 47-yard missed attempt.

When Northcutt returned the first punt of the second half 59 yards and three plays later caught a 15-yard touchdown pass from Holcomb, the Steelers' chances seemed as gray as the skies. They trailed 24-7.

Chris Fuamatu-Ma'afala runs in a game against the Browns.

"You get nervous," said halfback Jerome Bettis, who gave way to Amos Zereoue as the starter, "but there was no fear. There's a difference. Everybody's going to get nervous at times, but you find a way and that's what it's all about."

The Steelers found a way to cut the deficit to 10 points when Burress caught a 6-yard pass from Maddox, but Cleveland came right back with Dawson's 24-yard field goal for a 27-14 lead.

The Steelers cut it back to six on Maddox's 3-yard pass to Tuman but the Browns scored again to go up by 12. That set up the final, furious, successful Steelers comeback.

"What a game," Cowher said. ✦

Cowher Power

REGULAR SEASON (10-5-1)

Date	Visitor		Home	
9/9/2002	Steelers	14	Patriots	30
9/15/2002	Raiders	30	Steelers	17
9/29/2002	Browns	13	Steelers	16*
10/6/2002	Steelers	29	Saints	32
10/13/2002	Steelers	34	Bengals	7
10/21/2002	Colts	10	Steelers	28
10/27/2002	Steelers	31	Ravens	18
11/3/2002	Steelers	23	Browns	20

Date	Visitor		Home	
11/10/2002	Falcons	34	Steelers	34*
11/17/2002	Steelers	23	Titans	31
11/24/2002	Bengals	21	Steelers	29
12/1/2002	Steelers	25	Jaguars	23
12/8/2002	Texans	24	Steelers	6
12/15/2002	Panthers	14	Steelers	30
12/23/2002	Steelers	17	Buccaneers	7
12/29/2002	Ravens	31	Steelers	34

*Overtime

PLAYOFFS

Date	Visitor		Home	
1/5/2003	Browns	33	Steelers	36
1/11/2003	Steelers	31	Titans	34

INDIVIDUAL STATS

PASSING

Name	COM	ATT	PCT	YDS	YPA	TDs	INT	Sacks	Rating
Maddox	234	377	62.1%	2836	7.5	20	16	26	85.2
Stewart	109	166	65.7%	1155	7.0	6	6	7	82.8
Randle El	7	8	87.5%	45	5.6	0	0	1	90.1

PUNTING

Name	ATT	YDS	Inside 20
Miller	55	2267	14
Rouen	7	316	1

KICKING

Name	XP	XPA	FG	FGA	Points
Peterson	25	26	12	21	61
Reed	10	11	17	19	61

RUSHING

Name	ATT	YDS	AVG	TDs
Zereoue	193	762	3.9	4
Bettis	187	666	3.6	9
Stewart	43	191	4.4	2
Ward	12	142	11.8	0
Randle El	19	134	7.1	0
Fuamatu-Ma'afala	23	115	5.0	0
Haynes	10	51	5.1	0
Maddox	19	43	2.3	0
Kreider	6	16	2.7	0

RECEIVING

Name	REC	YDS	AVG	TDs
Ward	112	1329	11.9	12
Burress	78	1325	17.0	7
Randle El	47	489	10.4	2
Zereoue	42	341	8.1	0
Mathis	23	218	9.5	2
Kreider	18	122	6.8	1
Bruener	13	66	5.1	1
Bettis	7	57	8.1	0
Tuman	4	63	15.8	1
Haynes	3	10	3.3	0
Fuamatu-Ma'afala	2	12	6.0	0
Cushing	1	4	4.0	0

INTERCEPTIONS

Name	INT
Porter	4
Alexander	4
Washington	3
Townsend	3
Flowers	2
Scott	2
Logan	2

SACKS

Name	Sacks
Porter	9.0
Gildon	9.0
Haggans	6.5
Bailey	5.5
Smith	5.5
Flowers	4.0
K.Bell	4.0
von Oelhoffen	3.0
Hampton	2.0
Alexander	1.0
Logan	0.5

2003

Going For Paydirt

Steelers hope to strike it rich by adding a nickel to their dime

By Ed Bouchette, Post-Gazette Sports Writer

The Steelers will go back in time to try to improve their defense in the 2003 season. They can't bring back Joe Greene, Rod Woodson or Carnell Lake, so they will resurrect something else: The nickel defense.

It has been all the rage with the Steelers since they introduced it in the off-season. It's as if drivers suddenly discovered the Volkswagen Beetle. Like the Beetle, the nickel defense has been around for decades. It just hasn't been run in Pittsburgh for a while.

The reason wasn't so much that Coach Bill Cowher was out of touch, but that he had the personnel that rendered the nickel defense unnecessary.

Then his personnel changed, and the unit was exploited by offenses last season. Cowher and Tim Lewis, his defensive coordinator, opted to counter that by going back in time, back when a nickel really was a nickel.

"It's a response to what we've seen and what we're anticipating," Lewis said.

Defensive schemes can be confusing with players running in and out when situations on the field change. But the basic plans for each of the Steelers' three primary defenses are these:

• The Okie, or 3-4 base defense: Three down linemen, four linebackers (two in the middle and two outside the ends), four defensive backs.

• The dime defense: Four down linemen (usually including two linebackers who go into a three-point stance at end), one middle linebacker, six defensive backs.

• The nickel defense: Four down linemen (including the two linebackers), two inside linebackers, five defensive backs.

Before they revived the nickel, the Steelers went directly from their 3-4 to the dime in passing situations. Sometimes, that would mean six defensive backs on third-and-2 when an offense deployed four receivers.

Last year, when the Steelers brought in six defensive backs on third down, offenses often ran the ball. Or, they would spread the Steelers out by sending a back and a tight end wide, then shift them in tight and run the ball. It left the Steelers more vulnerable against the run because of the number of smaller defensive backs on the field.

This season, the Steelers likely will counter those situations with the nickel, which is more flexible against the run and the pass.

"The nickel is kind of a 'tweener for those situations," free safety Brent Alexander said. "Yeah, it does not have the same speed as the dime does, but it's not the base package, either."

Peter Diana

Amos Zereoue breaks away from the Browns' Lewis Sanders.

Peter Diana

Hines Ward falls down and slides past Jets' cornerback Ray Mickens.

"Mostly it is personnel," Cowher said. "Certainly, if they come out in four wide receivers, playing the nickel gives you some matchup problems. When there are three cover corners and they have four receivers, it limits you to what you can do.

"Not all teams are into using four receivers. You get a lot of three receivers, a tight end and a back, so now you have some flexibility with the nickel. You can play the nickel on down and distance. In second-and-long, you can go to the nickel because you can pick up more coverage flexibility. A lot of it will be predicated by down and distance and the personnel that is on the field."

As with their base defense, the nickel and dime are set up for linebackers to make plays, whether in the pass rush, stopping the run or pass coverage.

The nickel gets them even more involved. In the dime defense, two outside linebackers become defensive ends and rush the passer. One linebacker plays the middle. In the nickel, two linebackers play in the middle with one fewer defensive back behind them. The nickel keeps Kendrell Bell and James Farrior in the middle, just as they are in the 3-4 defense. In the dime defense last season, they both came off the field. Although Bell is supposed to play right rush end in the dime (Clark Haggans played there last year), many believe his best and most comfortable spot is inside, which is where he will play in the nickel. In that defense, Bell can rush the quarterback from any number of spots and do so standing up, not from a three-point stance on the outside.

Either way, the linebackers are the key. Jason Gildon, Joey Porter and Bell – all have made the Pro Bowl – play on all three defenses.

Peter Diana

Jerome Bettis is stopped by Ravens linebacker Ray Lewis in Baltimore.

Peter Diana

Hines Ward tries to haul in a tough catch against the 49ers' Ahmed Plummer in San Francisco.

"Guys who develop as defensive ends and linebackers have the ability to stand up, put their hand down, drop into coverage, match receivers, match running backs, match tight ends in man-to-man coverage, understand zone concepts," Lewis said. "It's a big key to what we do."

Here are situations in which the Steelers might deploy their various defenses:

- First-and-10. Base defense.
- Second-and-7, third-and-3. Nickel defense.
- Third-and-10 or longer. Dime defense.

Also, when opponents run the hurry-up offense, Cowher no longer has to choose between his base defense or his passing defense. Now he can send in the nickel because of its versatility against the run or the pass.

"The nickel gives you an opportunity to match up vs. personnel groupings that give the offense flexibilities to do that, or to stay in the traditional run set and run the football," Lewis said. "So, it's kind of a combination run-pass defensive package."

In the past, the Steelers would go to the dime defense in those 'tweener situations because they had big strong safeties such as Lake and Lee Flowers, not to mention bigger corners like Woodson.

"We had Carnell Lake, who could cover like a defensive back," Cowher said. "We would rather bring in the athletes who we could blitz with and who would give us flexibility in coverage than leave our base 3-4 defense on the field. A lot of times when we would go to the dime, we thought that the extra guy we brought on was just as good as a linebacker."

Now they believe Bell has the speed to cover when he has to, to blitz and to stop the run.

Jason Gildon complained early last season that the Steelers had gotten away from what they were doing when teams went to the spread offense. The nickel defense might be the answer to that problem.

"When I made that comment last year, it was just from the standpoint that I felt we were doing a lot of adjusting to teams rather than playing our defense and having them adjust to us," Gildon said. "I think the nickel is something we've been wanting to implement defensively. I think they finally feel comfortable with it now." ✦

2003 Game Of The Year:

A Long, Strange Night

Steelers and Ravens stage a finale flush with NFL history and histrionics

By Ed Bouchette, Post-Gazette Sports Writer

Jerome Bettis passed Jim Brown, Jamal Lewis passed 2,000 yards, and Josh Miller passed for one of the most bizarre touchdowns in Steelers history.

With nothing riding on the outcome, the Steelers and Baltimore Ravens staged an entertaining – and long – finale to the NFL regular season last night that included trick plays, strange plays, brutal hits, a pregame shouting match between Joey Porter and Ray Lewis and two backs carving out some NFL history.

The game and the Steelers' season ended in overtime when Matt Stover kicked a 47-yard field goal with 11:32 left in the extra period to give Baltimore a 13-10 victory. The loss concluded the Steelers' season at 6-10, tying their worst record under coach Bill Cowher. Baltimore improved to 10-6.

The outcome was rendered meaningless for playoff purposes when Cleveland upset Cincinnati in the afternoon. The loss by the Bengals gave the Ravens the AFC North championship, their first division title since the franchise moved to Baltimore from Cleveland in 1996.

Even though his team opens the playoffs Saturday at home against Tennessee, Baltimore coach Brian Billick did not use the opportunity to rest any starters last night. That included Jamal Lewis, who played the whole game and ran for 114 yards on 27 carries.

"This is the Pittsburgh Steelers, this is a rivalry," Billick said, explaining why he went full-tilt with his frontline players. "You can't cheat the game and you can't cheat the fans and who do you pull out? ... You play the game straight-up, because that's the way it's supposed to be."

In a strong year for running backs in the NFL, the Steelers' Bettis surpassed Hall of Famer Jim Brown for sixth on the career rushing list and Lewis became only the fifth player to rush for 2,000 yards in a season.

Bettis ran for 54 yards on 23 carries to give him 12,353 career rushing yards in what might have been his final game with the Steelers.

"For a player, it's once in a lifetime," Bettis said. "It's an honor just to pass a guy like that who's arguably the greatest running back to ever play."

Lewis finished the season with 2,066 yards, the second-best rushing year of any back in history. He fell short of Eric Dickerson's NFL-record 2,105 yards rushing, set in 1984.

"Second-leading all-time! That ain't bad," Billick said. "Came up short, but that's not a real priority for us. You make a hell of a run at it and it is what it is."

Lewis drew first blood with a 25-yard touchdown run in the first quarter. The Steelers drew up a play in the sand to tie it. Miller went back to punt; instead, he flipped a short pass to safety Chris Hope, who bobbed and weaved 81 yards for a touchdown in the third quarter.

"I guess it was that obvious that we could get away with it, and it worked out very well," Miller said.

The kickers then traded field goals with Jeff Reed making a 42-yarder and Stover scoring from 46.

Hines Ward caught only two passes to finish with 95 receptions and lose his grip on the AFC lead as the Ravens swarmed all over quarterback Tommy Maddox and the Steelers' offense. Maddox was sacked five times, threw three interceptions and lost a fumble. He completed 14 of 27 passes for 108 yards and had a passer rating of 22.4.

Jamal Lewis gained 39 yards on his first five carries on the first series of the game. His fifth carry gained 3 yards to give Baltimore a second-and-7 at the Steelers' 10. For some reason, Lewis was pulled from the game and backup Chester Taylor came in and carried for no gain. Anthony Wright then threw a fade pass into the right corner of the end zone for tight end Todd Heap. Deshea Townsend played it beautifully, leaped in front of Heap and came down with the interception

Ed Reed returned the favor two plays later when Maddox threw into double-coverage for Ward. Reed easily made the interception to give the Ravens the ball at the Steelers' 34.

On first down, Lewis ran off the right side for 9 yards, giving him 2,000 for the season. On second down, Lewis ran off the left side untouched for a 25-yard touchdown and a 7-0 Baltimore lead midway through the first quarter.

"Once we made some adjustments in the second quarter, I think we did well," Cowher said.

Lewis was making headway on the NFL record while Bettis found the going tougher to catch Brown. Bettis had only 3 yards on four carries after the first two series. But a 7-yard

Peter Diana

Kendrell Bell follows the block of teammate Clark Haggans during an interception return.

Lewis, and the Ravens had a first down at the Steelers' 10.

But Jamal Lewis lost a fumble on first down when Porter held him up and safety Brent Alexander plowed into him to pop the ball loose. Safety Mike Logan recovered at the 10.

That series of events led to one of the longest and strangest touchdown passes in Steelers history. On fourth-and-1 from the 19, Miller went back to punt, then flipped a short pass to Hope at the 14. Hope ran and ran and ran, criss-crossing through Baltimore's punt-return team to complete an 81-yard touchdown play to tie the score with 7:45 left in the third quarter.

It was the ninth-longest touchdown pass in Steelers history, and, by far, the longest thrown by a punter and the longest caught by a safety.

"I give Bill Cowher a hell of a lot of credit," Billick said. "That's a hell of a time to do the fake punt."

run in the second quarter gave him 13 yards and a tie with Brown for sixth place on the NFL's all-time rushing list. Brown had 12,312 yards, which led the NFL in career rushing until Walter Payton passed him in 1984.

On the next series, Bettis put Brown behind him with a 2-yard run.

Baltimore maintained its 7-0 lead at the half and Lewis already had 77 yards rushing on 11 carries. The Steelers held him to 69 yards rushing on 15 carries in the opener.

Maddox threw a second interception in the third quarter when, for the fifth time, one of his passes was tipped, this time by Hartwell. The ball glanced into the hands of Ray

Reed gave the Steelers their first lead, 10-7, when he made a 42-yard field goal with 2:30 to go in the third quarter. Bettis carried five of the six plays on that short drive, and the sixth kept the series going when the Ravens were penalized on third down for illegal hands to the face.

Stover tied it when he kicked a 46-yard field goal with 13:35 to play.

Cowher eschewed what would have been a 52-yard field-goal try to break the tie four minutes later. Instead, Maddox dropped back to pass and fumbled when he was hit by safety Chad Williams.

Baltimore had a chance to win it in regulation with two long field-goal tries in the final two minutes, but both were short – Stover from 52 and kickoff man Wade Richey from 51. ✦

Cowher Power

REGULAR SEASON (6-10)

Date	Visitor		Home		Date	Visitor		Home	
9/7/2003	Ravens	15	Steelers	34	11/9/2003	Cardinals	15	Steelers	28
9/14/2003	Steelers	20	Chiefs	41	11/17/2003	Steelers	14	49ers	30
9/21/2003	Steelers	17	Bengals	10	11/23/2003	Steelers	13	Browns	6
9/28/2003	Titans	30	Steelers	13	11/30/2003	Bengals	24	Steelers	20
10/5/2003	Browns	33	Steelers	13	12/7/2003	Raiders	7	Steelers	27
10/12/2003	Steelers	14	Broncos	17	12/14/2003	Steelers	0	Jets	6
10/26/2003	Rams	33	Steelers	21	12/21/2003	Chargers	24	Steelers	40
11/2/2003	Steelers	16	Seahawks	23	12/28/2003	Steelers	10	Ravens	13 *

*OT

INDIVIDUAL STATS

PASSING

Name	ATT	COM	PCT	YDS	YPA	TDs	INT	Sacks	Rating
Maddox	298	519	57.4	3414	6.6	18	17	41	75.3
Miller	1	1	100.0	81	81.0	1	0	0	158.3
Batch	4	8	50.0	47	5.9	0	0	1	68.2
Randle El	3	4	75.0	6	1.5	0	0	0	77.1

PUNTING

Name	ATT	YDS	Inside 20
Miller	84	3521	27

KICKING

Name	XP	XPA	FG	FGA	Points
Reed	31	32	23	32	100

RUSHING

Name	ATT	YDS	AVG	TDs
Bettis	246	811	3.3	7
Zereoue	132	433	3.3	2
Randle El	15	75	5.0	0
Haynes	20	63	3.2	0
Ward	11	61	5.5	0
Kreider	7	29	4.1	1
Maddox	13	12	0.9	0
Batch	1	11	11.0	0
Burress	1	-7	-7.0	0

RECEIVING

Name	REC	YDS	AVG	TDs
Ward	95	1163	12.2	10
Burress	60	860	14.3	4
Zereoue	40	310	7.8	0
Randle El	37	364	9.8	1
Doering	18	240	13.3	1
Bettis	13	86	6.6	0
Tuman	12	113	9.4	0
Riemersma	10	138	13.8	1
Kreider	9	107	11.9	0
Haynes	7	57	8.1	0
Mays	2	17	8.5	0
Bruener	2	12	6.0	1
Hope	1	81	81.0	1

INTERCEPTIONS

Name	INT
Alexander	4
Scott	3
Townsend	3
Bell	1
Farrior	1
Washington	1
Gildon	1

SACKS

Name	Sacks
von Oelhoffen	8.0
Gildon	6.0
Porter	5.0
Bell	4.0
Bailey	2.0
Polamalu	2.0
A. Smith	2.0
Alexander	1.0
Haggans	1.0
Hampton	1.0
Logan	1.0
Townsend	1.0

2004

What's Old Is New Again

The 3-4 defense is back in vogue

By Ed Bouchette, Post-Gazette Sports Writer

The 3-4 defense was as rare in the NFL as the straight-on kicker several years ago. Only one team used a three-man line as its base of operations and that was right here in Pittsburgh

Two of those defenses will open the 2004 season in Heinz Field when the Oakland Raiders play the Steelers, and the 3-4 is popping up faster than Krispy Kreme Donut shops. The popular defense of the 1980s that neared extinction in the 1990s is back in full force.

Oakland and San Diego in the past few years joined other converts like Houston, Baltimore and New England in adopting the 3-4 defense. That makes six teams, counting the Steelers, that deploy that defense primarily. Others beginning to use it as part of their package are Dallas, San Francisco, the New York Jets and New Orleans. Ten teams, or nearly one third of the league, now use the 3-4 in some form.

"It is a very good defense," said Steelers end Kimo von Oelhoffen, who led the Steelers with eight sacks out of that defense last season. "If you have the right personnel, it's an excellent defense. It's a defense that limits a lot of what offenses can do. The 4-3 has been around so long that there are so many schemes to block it. It's tough to block the 3-4."

It was the Patriots who helped spawn the 3-4

comeback by using it last season on the way to a Super Bowl victory. But no one has had more continued success with the 3-4 defense than Bill Cowher, who installed it when he became Steelers coach in 1992, carrying on a tradition that Chuck Noll started when he broke up his old Steel Curtain and switched to the 3-4 in 1983.

Cowher's defenses ranked in the league's top 10 nine times in the past 11 seasons, including No. 1 in 2001 when the Steelers went 13-3 and reached the AFC championship game. Besides Cowher, no coach embraces the defense more enthusiastically than his coordinator, Dick LeBeau.

"It gives you more team speed and gives you four 240-pound men who can run who are in 2-point stances," LeBeau said. "And they can also see, so you can do a few more things with them, you can make more adjustments because they're standing up and watching, as opposed to the four down linemen in a 3-point stance and you have to convey all the changes to him down there."

The 3-4 consists of three down linemen – a nose tackle in the middle flanked by two ends. Two linebackers stand on the outside edge of the ends, with two inside linebackers and the traditional two cornerbacks and two safeties. Most teams, in passing situations, rush four players (five or more is considered a blitz). The linemen in the 4-3 are the tradi-

Cowher Power

Willie Williams is greeted by teammates after sacking Eagles quarterback Donovan McNabb.

Peter Diana

Peter Diana

Ben Roethlisberger escapes Ravens' defensive tackle Kelly Gregg to release a shovel pass to Jerome Bettis.

tional rushers, while the 3-4 rush the lineman and one linebacker. But which one?

"It's kind of a balanced set," von Oelhoffen said, "and it's really easy to disguise coverages, because you have four linebackers and three of them are covering. But you don't know which three. The safeties can disguise, the cornerbacks can disguise because of where the safety's at. It's just a good defense."

The 3-4 puts more emphasis on the linebackers to make the plays, particularly sacks, instead of the linemen.

"It expands your pressure abilities," LeBeau said, "because you have that fourth linebacker and it

gives you a little more element of surprise, because they have to guess a little bit about which of those four guys are coming.

"I think another plus of the 3-4 is there are more gifted 240-pound athletes [3-4 linebackers] than there are gifted 300-pound athletes [4-3 tackles]. So you open up a little more of the real outstanding college defensive end who is not quite big enough, he's just about right for the 3-4."

The 4-3 produced legendary fronts such as the Fearsome Foursome, Purple People Eaters, Doomsday Defense and, of course, the Steel Curtain. But the 3-4 helped produce Pro Bowl linebackers, at least around these parts, such as Mike Merriweather, Greg Lloyd, Kevin Greene, Chad Brown, Jason Gildon and Joey Porter.

The Steelers put an outside linebacker in the Pro

Cowher Power

Bill Cowher throws to the receivers during training camp drills.

Bill Cowher greets Jerome Bettis after the running back scores a touchdown against the Jets.

Bowl nine of the 12 years under Cowher. Part of that reason may be the fact Pro Bowl voters use sacks to help determine the best players. The outside linebackers in the 3-4 have a big advantage in that area over their counterparts in the 4-3, where outside linebackers cover receivers more than rush the quarterback. Traditionally, 3-4 outside linebackers play end in nickel and dime passing defenses.

Conversely, the 3-4 ends get short shrift in the voting. No Steelers defensive end made a Pro Bowl since L.C. Greenwood, following the Steeler's last Super Bowl victory in the 1979 season, when they used the 4-3 defense.

The Steelers' line, though, has been a good one, particularly over the past two seasons.

"I think one of the real strengths of our defense is our defensive line," LeBeau said.

Von Oelhoffen became the first end to lead them in sacks since Tim Johnson had four in 1988. Nose tackle Casey Hampton made the past Pro Bowl. Left end Aaron Smith is one of their highest-paid players because he's outstanding against the run and he pushes the pocket, forcing the quarterback to run into the arms of the linebackers.

LeBeau has seen it all in his 45 years in the NFL, including 14 as a player with the Detroit Lions; he's not surprised at the comeback of the 3-4 defense. When he first came into the league, everyone played a four-man front, but the merger in 1970 brought more 3-4 defenses from the AFC and things began to change. They moved back to the 4-3, and now the pendulum is swinging back toward the three-man front.

Coaches love to tinker, but then "If you get a real good bunch of defensive players," LeBeau said, "they're probably going to do all right for you no matter what scheme you put them in." ✦

2004 Game Of The Year:

There's No Place Like Home

Steelers add Eagles to string of impressive wins at Heinz Field

By Ed Bouchette, Post-Gazette Sports Writer

With 34 players from their last Super Bowl championship watching, the Steelers planted another stake in the Heinz Field turf, claiming the high ground in the NFL as theirs and theirs alone.

They not only beat the last perfect team in the NFL one week after beating the last perfect team in the AFC, but also dispatched the Philadelphia Eagles with such ease that they looked to be in a league of their own.

No team in NFL history had taken out unbeaten teams in consecutive weeks this late in the season, but the Steelers accomplished that by ripping the Eagles, 27-3, one week after sandbagging New England's 21-game unbeaten streak.

It left the Steelers tied for the NFL's best record with Philadelphia and New England at 7-1 but, after such dominance the past two Sundays, it left few doubting which team is king of the NFL hill halfway through the season.

"We're playing the best, obviously," said center Jeff Hartings. "We beat the best team in the AFC, the best team in the NFC. That's not to toot our own horn. The pundits are going to do that, anyway."

Once again, the Steelers did it after losing one of their key starters. The week before, they bludgeoned the Patriots 34-20 without Pro Bowl nose tackle Casey Hampton and cornerback Chad Scott. Yesterday, they played without Duce Staley, the AFC's third-leading rusher who was so pumped up to play his former team that he tried to convince coach Bill Cowher to play him despite a hamstring injury.

Cowher decided to save him from further injury and went to the bullpen, where Jerome Bettis came out and blew away the Eagles. Bettis ran 33 times – his busiest workload in four years – and gained 149 yards behind gaping holes created by his line.

"It boggles me that people were concerned that Duce was not in there, and 'What were we going to do?' " Bettis said. "I have been getting it done for a long time."

The Steelers scored touchdowns on their first three possessions for a 21-0 lead, and the battle for Pennsylvania looked more like the Little Big Horn.

Receiver Hines Ward scored touchdowns on a 16-yard end-around – his first NFL rushing touchdown – and a 20-yard pass from quarterback Ben Roethlisberger, who tied the modern NFL record with his 6-0 start by a rookie.

After each score, Ward imitated Eagles receiver Terrell Owen's arm-flapping-Eagle touchdown dance. Ward said he was just having fun.

"We're 7-1 right now, halfway through the year," Ward said. "That's a great feeling."

Roethlisberger then threw a 2-yard touchdown pass to tight end Jay Riemersma after rolling to the right and appearing ready to run for the score. That made it 21-0, and the rest was anticlimactic as David Akers scored Philadelphia's only points with a 33-yard field goal and Jeff Reed scored the only points of the second half with field goals from 42 and 31 yards.

"I have no doubt that the red target will be on our chest now," said linebacker Joey Porter.

Porter and the defense dominated Owens, quarterback Donovan McNabb and the rest of Philadelphia's offense. The Steelers piled up 420 yards to the Eagles' 113, had 25 first downs to Philadelphia's seven and converted 8 of 15 third downs while Philadelphia was 0 for 8. Chris Gardocki did not punt, marking the first time in Steelers history that happened.

The Eagles, who have reached the past three NFC championships, had won their previous nine road games.

"They beat us up in every phase of the game," Eagles coach Andy Reid said. "Starting with the coaches, then to the offense, the defense and then to our special teams. They were the better team today, and they deserve the credit."

The Steelers sacked McNabb four times, intercepted one pass and held him to 109 yards, third-lowest output of his career. He completed 15 of 24 passes and had a 55.7 passer rating. Owens, the NFL leader in touchdown catches with nine, was blanked on that end and averaged only 7.6 yards on his seven catches for 53 yards.

"We couldn't let him sit back there and have time," Cowher said of the many blitzes the Steelers threw at McNabb. "He is just going to pick you apart. We tried to fill up all the lanes by rushing him and blitzing him."

McNabb, one of the NFL's best running quarterbacks, did not have a rushing attempt. But then, few other Eagles did, either. Brian Westbrook, playing with a broken rib, ran six

James Farrior intercepts a pass from the Eagles' Donovan McNabb.

times, and the Eagles ran nine times in total for only 23 yards.

Coupled with the Patriots' 5 yards rushing last week, that's 28 yards rushing against the Steelers in the past two games.

The Steelers, on the other hand, ran 56 times, four short of their team record, for 252 yards, including Verron Haynes' 51.

Roethlisberger threw an interception for only the second time in his past 134 attempts, but he otherwise was near-perfect. He completed 11 of 18 passes for 183 yards and two touchdowns and a 109.3 passer rating. He also ran 16 yards on third-and-13 to keep the first scoring drive going.

"It was just one of those games where everybody stepped up and there was somebody different every play," said Porter.

Four players had sacks – cornerback Willie Williams and linebackers James Farrior, Clark Haggans and Larry Foote – and Farrior also intercepted a McNabb pass and returned it 41 yards.

The Steelers' dominance was complete and, after beating the best the league had to offer in successive weeks, they have become the team to beat for everyone else.

"We're definitely not home free. We have a veteran group here. We're not going to get ahead of ourselves. A lot of us have been through that 2001 season, and that hurdle made us understand it's not over until you reach your goal," Hartings said, referring to the Steelers' upset loss in the AFC championship game three years ago. "So, we're pretty much levelheaded."

And they're pretty much on a level by themselves at the moment. ✦

Cowher Power

REGULAR SEASON (10-6)

Date	Visitor		Home		Date	Visitor		Home	
9/12/2004	Raiders	21	Steelers	24	11/14/2004	Steelers	24	Browns	10
9/19/2004	Steelers	13	Ravens	30	11/21/2004	Steelers	19	Bengals	14
9/26/2004	Steelers	13	Dolphins	3	11/28/2004	Redskins	7	Steelers	16
10/3/2004	Bengals	17	Steelers	28	12/5/2004	Steelers	17	Jaguars	16
10/10/2004	Browns	23	Steelers	34	12/12/2004	Jets	6	Steelers	17
10/17/2004	Steelers	24	Cowboys	20	12/18/2004	Steelers	33	Giants	30
10/31/2004	Patriots	20	Steelers	34	12/26/2004	Ravens	7	Steelers	20
11/7/2004	Eagles	3	Steelers	27	1/2/2005	Steelers	29	Bills	24

PLAYOFFS

Date	Visitor		Home	
1/15/2005	Jets	17	Steelers	20 *
1/23/2005	Patriots	41	Steelers	27

*OT

INDIVIDUAL STATS

PASSING

Name	COM	ATT	PCT	YDS	YPA	TDs	INT	Sacks	Rating
Roethlisberger	196	295	66.4	2621	8.88	17	11	30	98.1
Maddox	30	60	50.0	329	5.48	1	2	6	58.3
Bettis	1	1	100.0	10	10.00	1	0	0	147.9
Randle El	1	1	100.0	10	10.00	1	0	0	147.9
St. Pierre	0	1	0.0	0	0.00	0	0	0	39.6

PUNTING

Name	ATT	YDS	Inside 20
Gardocki	67	2879	24

KICKING

Name	XP	XPA	FG	FGA	Points
Reed	40	40	28	33	124

RUSHING

Name	ATT	YDS	AVG	TDs
Bettis	250	941	3.8	13
Staley	192	830	4.3	1
Haynes	55	272	4.9	0
Parker	32	186	5.8	0
Roethlisberger	56	144	2.6	1
Randle El	8	34	4.3	0
Ward	7	25	3.6	1
Kreider	4	18	4.5	0
Maddox	9	15	1.7	0
Brown	1	2	2.0	0
St. Pierre	4	-3	-.7	0

RECEIVING

Name	REC	YDS	AVG	TDs
Ward	80	1004	12.6	4
Randle El	43	601	14.0	3
Burress	35	698	19.9	5
Haynes	18	142	7.9	2
Kreider	10	75	7.5	1
Mays	9	137	15.2	0
Tuman	9	89	9.9	3
Riemersma	7	82	11.7	2
Staley	6	55	9.2	0
Bettis	6	46	7.7	0
Parker	3	16	5.3	0
Cushing	1	17	17.0	0
Morey	1	8	8.0	0

INTERCEPTIONS

Name	INT
Polamalu	5
Farrior	4
Townsend	4
Hope	1
Scott	1
Porter	1
Foote	1
I. Taylor	1
Williams	1

SACKS

Name	Sacks
A. Smith	8
Porter	7
Haggans	6
Townsend	4
Farrior	3
Foote	3
Colclough	1
Harrison	1
Hoke	1
Kirschke	1
Polamalu	1
von Oelhoffen	1
Williams	1
Kriewaldt	0

Facing The Music

No longer a rookie, Roethlisberger has discovered the price of fame & high expectations

By Ed Bouchette, Post-Gazette Sports Writer

Ben Roethlisberger sits in your movie theater, shops at your local supermarket, dines in your restaurants, dates your women. He swoops up and down your highways on his Harley and bar-hops on the South Side.

He just cannot do those things around Pittsburgh the way he did a year ago.

He came to the Steelers as Big Ben in April 2004, and became Colossal Ben not long into his rookie season. Today? He's Dan Marino II, author of the greatest rookie season by a quarterback, the first quarterback to win 13 starts without a loss in a season.

And now look at what you've done, fella. You went out and created one fine mess for yourself. No more waiting in lines at the movie theatre, that's for sure.

"I have to go when the movies start, when it's dark," Roethlisberger said, "and rise and leave early, toward the end. Even then it can still be tough."

Grocery shopping's just no fun at all. He and a friend race up and down the aisles, tossing food in a cart as if he's running the two-minute drill.

"We do it real quick. I go grocery shopping once a month now instead of once every couple of weeks. My grocery bill is real big because I just stock up. You'd think I was stocking up for the winter."

Steelers halfback Verron Haynes, his roommate in camp and on the road, knows there's no such thing as a leisurely night out in a restaurant with Big Ben.

"It's interesting because he can't even get a bite of his meal when we're out eating dinner," said Haynes, laughing. "But I guess that comes with the territory. It's kind of one of those things you take on when you're the starting quarterback."

Surely, though, Trent Dilfer does not go through this in Cleveland. Quarterbacks have swayed between notorious and famous in Pittsburgh, but perhaps only Terry Bradshaw attracted the attention that comes with being Big Ben. None certainly would cause local television stations to break into their news with reports that he was "injured" in practice – as has happened twice already with Roethlisberger – when he was only bruised.

But if you think his celebrity is large now, just wait, for his aspirations dwarf it all.

"Win Super Bowls, especially for this city," Roethlisberger said, running through his grocery list.

And?

"I'd like to be the best ever to play the game, in the group when they think 'Montana, Elway and Marino,' they say my name in there."

Anything else?

"And I want to be a first-ballot Hall of Famer."

First, there's this little matter of playing his second season in the National Football League. Some have used the phrases "sophomore jinx" or "sophomore slump" to describe what could happen to

Cowher Power

Peter Diana

Hines Ward extends for a ball and makes the catch against the Browns' Leigh Bodden.

Matt Freed

Troy Polamalu and teammate Ike Taylor upend the Colts' Bryan Fletcher.

"Are there ways to get better? Yes, absolutely. He's going to try to fine-tune those and obviously you want to win the Super Bowl, so his expectations in his second year are kind of like what Marino's were. It's kind of like, all of a sudden, 'OK, you're there. It's time to win the big one now.' "

Batch feels sorry for 49ers rookie quarterback Alex Smith, this year's first draft choice.

"His expectations are going to be high because of what happened the previous year, because of what happened to Ben. That's going to be everybody for years to come. You don't just win your first 14 games, it just doesn't happen.

"It's like now everybody's comparing themselves as the next Ben Roethlisberger. Before, everybody was trying to say, 'Who's the next Marino?' "

In Roethlisberger's words, Marino has become a mentor to him. They've talked many times in the summer, in person, on the phone. Marino advises how to handle defenses as well as the news media and the public. Marino was a champ at thwarting all three, when necessary, with the quick release.

"It's tough," Roethlisberger says of dealing with the public, "because sometimes you get annoyed, you don't have a good day at practice, and it seems when we don't have good days, everybody wants to talk to you. Some days you're hurting and don't want to sign autographs. Or something's going on and you don't always want to deal with people.

"But what I try to remember – and Warren Moon told me this – if you don't feel like dealing with people and dealing with the hassles of being who you are, then don't go out. Don't put yourself in a position where you can be a jerk."

There have been instances in which he and coach

Roethlisberger in the 2005 season, as if every player who was successful as a rookie, slumped in his second year.

Marino did not, Peyton Manning did not. Few quarterbacks have had the chance at a sophomore slump because they hardly played as rookies – guys such as Carson Palmer and Tom Brady – or they did not play well as rookies, such as Bradshaw or Eli Manning.

Charlie Batch did. He started 12 games as a Detroit Lions rookie in 1998 and had a better season in 1999. Batch knows Roethlisberger's experience from last season can only help him in this one, but he also knows that his 2004 success will be difficult to top.

"I guess his question is, how do you move forward?" Batch said. "Nobody ever expected for him to do what he did. Now, it's kind of like, well, how can you get better?

Peter Diana

Jerome Bettis scores his second touchdown of the afternoon against the Bears at Heinz Field.

Bill Cowher seemed to regard each other as such over public disagreements such as Roethlisberger's riding his motorcycle without a helmet, or the quarterback's broken/no-they're-not-broken toes from the AFC championship game. Cowher called their relationship "very solid."

"Like anything else, it will grow with time and as we continue to go through ups and downs," Cowher said. "I'm always there for him, and he'll always know how I feel. We have a very trusting relationship."

Roethlisberger said it's the public and the media who put the wrong spin on otherwise minor issues between him and his coach.

"People speculated about the motorcycle thing and the helmet thing and people blew it up," Roethlisberger said. "And only he and I knew what was said, and there was not one bad thing that was said. I did not defy him at all, and I think we have a great relationship. And I would hope he says the same thing.

"When he asks me to do something, I'm going to do it to the best of my ability. And I feel I can go talk to him about things and he can talk to me and I hope our relationship will just continue to build."

Cowher even enjoys, somewhat, the rebel in his quarterback.

"He's a very confident, competitive person," Cowher said. "I think when you take guys who have those characteristics, they don't like to not have success.

"I've never had any issues with Ben. I certainly have talked to him sometimes about choices and consequences, the same thing you do with any other player. But I have never had any problems with him in terms of our communications and what his responses are, and that's all I can ask."

Cowher points to Roethlisberger's experience and success as a rookie, combined with his work in the offseason as reasons he believes he will continue his excellence this season. The two have talked about how defensive coordinators, especially those in the AFC North Division, likely spent extra time looking at him on tape this year.

"They certainly will look at his last few games where he probably didn't play as well as he did earlier," Cowher said of the two playoff contests. "At what was the common denominator and some of the things he did.

"I don't think it's a case where he has to rectify any one area. It's just recognition and being patient. I think that's the thing. He probably dealt with fatigue as the year went on, but I think now he knows what to expect. He went through it once and I think that will be a great benefit to him."

As then-Dolphins general manager, Rick Spielman saw Roethlisberger's first pro start in the wake of a hurricane-delayed game in Miami on Sept. 26, 2004. The rookie's first pass was intercepted that night, and he completed 12 of 22 passes for 163 yards. But it was his lone touchdown pass that most impressed Spielman.

Roethlisberger faked a pitch to Duce Staley from Miami's 7, dropped back and rolled to his right when he found no one open. He kept running and so did Hines Ward, and when Roethlisberger threw at the last second, Ward dove in front of the end zone to catch it for the only touchdown with 6:16 left in the Steelers 13-3 victory.

"From then on, each week he kept growing and growing, probably getting more confidence in himself," said Spielman, who now works for ESPN and spent a week watching the Steelers in training camp. "He's a year more mature. He's been through about everything. He's been in a pressure situation already as a rookie in a championship game. So I think he'll continue to grow and continue to improve and become one of the best quarterbacks in the league."

But, of course, Roethlisberger does not want to become just one of the best quarterbacks in the league.

"I plan on and want to be the best quarterback to ever play the game," Roethlisberger said. ✦

2005 Game Of The Year:
Whew!
Steelers hang on for victory

By Ed Bouchette

Move over Immaculate Reception, you have some company.

The Steelers head to Denver for the AFC championship in one week after their most improbable ending to a playoff game since Franco Harris ran into history in 1972.

They survived the Indianapolis Colts, 21-18, because quarterback Ben Roethlisberger made a game-saving tackle and Mike Vanderjagt, the most accurate field-goal kicker in NFL history, missed badly from 46 yards with 17 seconds left.

"I don't need too many more of those feelings," receiver Hines Ward said, "but it's good to come out on the right side. You thought the game was over, your season was over and then the guy missed the field goal."

The game appeared over when linebacker Joey Porter sacked quarterback Peyton Manning on fourth down at the Colts' 2 with 1:20 left and the Steelers ahead by three, the game's fifth sack of the NFL's leading passer.

Because the Colts had three timeouts left to stop the clock, the Steelers sent Jerome Bettis off right guard to try to put it away.

"We score there, and the game's over," coach Bill Cowher said.

But linebacker Gary Brackett slammed into Bettis and put his helmet on the ball. The man who rarely fumbles fumbled for the first time this season.

The ball popped backward. Cornerback Nick Harper, playing with three stitches in his right knee where his wife allegedly stabbed him the day before, picked it up. He had one man to beat to run 93 yards for the go-ahead touchdown – Roethlisberger.

"It's one of those things that once in a blue moon Jerome fumbles, and once in a blue moon I'm going to make that tackle," Roethlisberger said.

The quarterback who had not made a tackle in two NFL seasons got in front of Harper, wrestled with him a little and then tackled him by the foot as tight end Jerame Tuman came in to finish him off. For all the punishment the Steelers dealt to Manning and the Colts' offense, a tackle by their quarterback was the most important of all.

"That might be the biggest play ever in his career," linebacker Larry Foote said. "My heart was going to my feet and back up."

Still, the Colts and Manning had the ball at their 42 with 1:01 left. They reached the Steelers' 28, where rookie cornerback Bryant McFadden broke up a pass in the end zone to Reggie Wayne on second down and knocked away another for Wayne on third.

Vanderjagt came on to do what he does better than anyone: Convert a field goal and send it to overtime.

"Not today," Foote said.

Vanderjagt's attempt was long enough, but looked to be 20 feet wide, and the Steelers became the first No. 6 playoff seed to knock off a No. 1 seed.

"That was one of the craziest games I have been in," Porter said. "It feels good for the ball to actually bounce our way one time."

The Steelers, winning for the sixth consecutive time, overcame 10-point odds to a team that beat them, 26-7, here Nov. 28. The Colts were favorites to win the Super Bowl.

"A day ago, nobody wanted to give us a chance," Ward said. "We came out and we did what we had to do. We knew it would be tough to come into Indianapolis, and they beat us pretty good the last time. This is kind of redemption for us."

The Steelers stunned the Colts and the noisy RCA Dome crowd when they took a 14-0 lead in the first quarter on Roethlisberger's touchdown passes of 6 yards to Antwaan Randle El and 7 to rookie Heath Miller.

Roethlisberger was hot, hitting 6 of 7 on the first scoring drive and connecting with Ward for a 45-yard pass on third-down that set up the second touchdown. He would throw only five times in the second half, completing 14 of 24 on the day for 197 yards.

"We knew we wanted to do that early on and establish at that point that we were going to throw the ball on our own terms," Miller said.

When many expected the Steelers to run and control the clock, they came out throwing. They ran 13 times in the first half, and Roethlisberger threw 19 times and completed 12 in the first two quarters as the Colts dropped one safety back and kept everyone else but their cornerbacks close to the line of scrimmage.

"I knew they were going to give us eight guys in the box,"

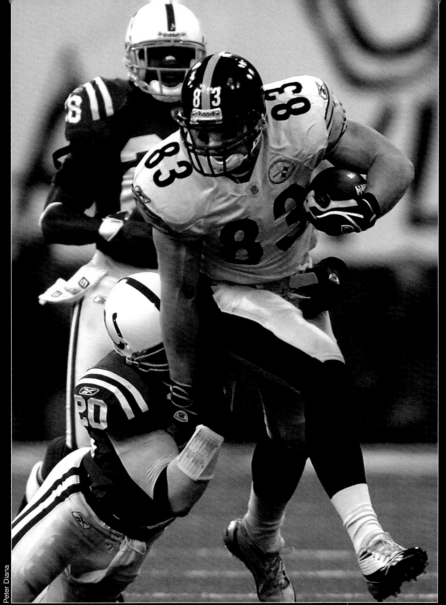

Peter Diana

aged only Vanderjagt's 20-yard field goal in the first half.

"I think we pressured them a lot more," Foote said. "Coach [Dick] LeBeau whipped up some new magic, gave them something nobody's seen yet."

The Steelers seemed poised to put the game away after linebacker James Farrior's booming sack on a blitz of Manning put the ball on the Colts' 1 on fourth down. The Steelers took over on the Indianapolis 30 after the punt and ran six times in a row – Willie Parker on an 11-yard scoot to start it and then Bettis five times for the other 19, including the final one up the middle for a touchdown that bounced them in front, 21-3.

Cowher's record is 100-1-1 in the regular season when his team leads at any point by more than 10. That did not seem to be in jeopardy even when Manning threw a 50-yard touchdown pass to Dallas Clark early in the fourth quarter.

And safety Troy Polamalu appeared to settle matters when he made a diving interception of Manning at the Steelers' 48 with 5:26 left.

But Colts coach Tony Dungy challenged it, and referee Pete Morelli overturned it, saying Polamalu dropped it, even though he did not drop it until he stood up after making the catch and before a Colts player touched him.

The Steelers were incensed by the call. (The NFL later admitted that the referee erred.)

"The world wanted Indy to win so bad, they were going to do whatever they had to do, man," Porter claimed. "It was like the 9-1-1 year, when they wanted the [New England] Patriots to win it for the world ... At a point, I didn't think the refs were going to let us get out of here with a victory."

The Colts, given new life, continued on the series that ended with Edgerrin James' running 3 yards for a touchdown. Manning's pass to Wayne for the two-point conversion drew the Colts to within three with 4:24 left, and the Dome rocked again.

When Porter sacked Manning twice in three plays, dropping him at the 2 on fourth down, it was all over. Except for a few plays at the end.

"I know a couple of times our players were ready to celebrate prematurely," Cowher said.

That they finally got to do so was a wonder in itself. ✦

Heath Miller breaks away from the Colts' Mike Doss in Indianapolis.

coordinator Ken Whisenhunt said, "and they were going to play to stop the run. And our quarterback is really maturing, and he's understanding what we're trying to do."

Roethlisberger threw his only interception, in the first half, when he was hit by Dwight Freeney. But the Colts did nothing with that, much the way they spent the first three quarters. Manning (22 of 38, 290) threw off target, his passes sailing on him. The Steelers seemed to rattle him with both their blitzes and their disguised non-blitzes. Indianapolis man-

Cowher Power

REGULAR SEASON (11-5)

Date	Visitor		Home		Date	Visitor		Home	
9/11/2005	Titans	7	Steelers	34	11/13/2005	Browns	21	Steelers	34
9/18/2005	Steelers	27	Texans	7	11/20/2005	Steelers	13	Ravens	16
9/25/2005	Patriots	23	Steelers	20	11/28/2005	Steelers	7	Colts	26
10/10/2005	Steelers	24	Chargers	22	12/4/2005	Bengals	38	Steelers	31
10/16/2005	Jaguars	23	Steelers	17	12/11/2005	Bears	9	Steelers	21
10/23/2005	Steelers	27	Bengals	13	12/18/2005	Steelers	18	Vikings	3
10/31/2005	Ravens	19	Steelers	20	12/24/2005	Steelers	41	Browns	0
11/6/2005	Steelers	20	Packers	10	1/1/2006	Lions	21	Steelers	35

*OT

PLAYOFFS

Date	Visitor		Home	
1/8/2006	Steelers	31	Bengals	17
1/15/2006	Steelers	21	Colts	18
1/22/2006	Steelers	34	Broncos	17
2/5/2006	Seahawks	10	Steelers	21

INDIVIDUAL STATS

PASSING

	ATT	COM	YDS	TD	INT	RATE
Roethlisberger	268	168	2385	17	9	98.6
Maddox	71	34	406	2	4	51.7
Batch	36	23	246	1	1	81.5
Randle El	3	3	67	1	0	158.3
Gardocki	1	0	0	0	0	39.6

PUNTING

	NO	YDS	AVG	20	LONG	BLK
Gardocki	67	2803	41.8	22	65	0
Roethlisberger	2	72	36.0	1	39	0

RUSHING

Name	ATT	YDS	AVG	TDs
Parker	255	1202	4.7	4
Bettis	110	368	3.3	9
Haynes	74	274	3.7	3
Staley	38	148	3.9	1
Randle El	12	73	6.1	0
Roethlisberger	31	69	2.2	3
Batch	11	30	2.7	1
Maddox	8	26	3.3	0
Kreider	3	21	7.0	0
Ward	3	10	3.3	0
Herron	3	2	0.7	0
Wilson	1	0	0.0	0

RECEIVING

Name	REC	YDS	AVG	TDs
Ward	69	975	14.1	11
Miller	39	459	11.8	6
Randle El	35	558	15.9	1
Wilson	26	451	17.3	0
Parker	18	218	12.1	1
Haynes	11	113	10.3	0
Morgan	9	150	16.7	2
Kreider	7	43	6.1	0
Staley	6	34	5.7	0
Bettis	4	40	10.0	0
Tuman	3	57	19.0	0
Kranchick	1	6	6.0	0
Morey	0	0	-	0

INTERCEPTIONS

Name	INT
Hope	3
Polamalu	2
Townsend	2
Porter	2
Harrison	1
Colclough	1
Carter	1
McFadden	1
A. Smith	1
Taylor	1

SACKS

Name	Sacks
Porter	10.5
Haggans	9.0
von Oelhoffen	3.5
Foote	3.0
Harrison	3.0
Keisel	3.0
Polamalu	3.0
Townsend	3.0
J. Farrior	2.0
A. Smith	2.0
Carter	1.0
Colclough	1.0
Frazier	1.0
Kirschke	1.0
McFadden	1.0

High Five

A Riveting run to glory

By Ed Bouchette, Post-Gazette Sports Writer

The Steelers' long search to repeat as Super Bowl champions ended after 26 years when they trumped the Seattle Seahawks, 21-10, at Ford Field.

Playing before a rollicking crowd dominated by Pittsburgh's black and gold, the Steelers won their fifth Vince Lombardi Trophy, tying the Dallas Cowboys and San Francisco 49ers for the most in the game's 40 years.

The Steelers capped a storybook run by winning their eighth consecutive game, became the first team to win three road playoff games and then the Super Bowl, and finished the Jerome Bettis saga in grand style.

"Our effort today made history," coach Bill Cowher said. "That's what made it special to me: This team has been real resilient all year. It was one guy after another. It's a tremendous group of guys."

Bettis, who rushed for 43 yards, raised the Lombardi Trophy and virtually announced his retirement in his hometown.

"I think the Bus' last stop is here in Detroit," Bettis told the crowd on the field after the game. "Detroit, you were incredible. Pittsburgh, here we come."

The Steelers flew home lugging their shiny, new silver booty to join the four trophies the franchise won in the 1970s.

"We're so proud to bring it back to Pittsburgh," Dan Rooney said.

Wide receiver Hines Ward, who began training camp with a contract holdout, won the game's Most Valuable Player award after catching five passes for 123 yards, including a 43-yard touchdown from fellow wide receiver Antwaan Randle El.

"This is the one for the thumb," Ward said, holding his young son and, as usual, smiling. "We are bringing the Super Bowl back to the City of Pittsburgh."

Quarterback Ben Roethlisberger, who threw two interceptions and had a miserable 22.6 passer rating, nevertheless made plays when his team needed them. He dived into the end zone on third down for a touchdown in the second quarter and picked up another key first down in the fourth. In all, he ran seven times for 25 yards but completed just 9 of 21 passes for 123 yards.

Seattle halfback Shaun Alexander, the league MVP, was held to 95 yards on 20 carries.

Steelers' halfback Willie Parker finished with 93 on 10 carries, most of that on one burst – a 75-yard touchdown run on the second play of the second half that was the longest in Super Bowl history and brought a 14-3 lead.

Parker ran a counter off the right. Pulling guard Alan Faneca, tackle Max Starks and guard Kendall

Matt Freed

Bettis is upended by Michael Boulware of the Seahawks.

Matt Freed

Simmons threw big blocks, and Parker swooped through the line and was gone. Safety Etric Pruitt, playing for injured starter Marquand Manuel, made a diving attempt at Seattle's 40 to no avail.

Parker lit into the end zone, and the place erupted in a Terrible Towel windstorm.

"I just knew it was going to be a great play," Parker said. "They called it at the right time, and Faneca just paved the way."

The Steelers held the Seahawks, then moved in for what looked to be a *coup de grace* with a first down at the Seattle 11. After two Bettis runs moved Pittsburgh to the 7, wide receiver Cedrick Wilson flashed open behind cornerback Kelly Herndon on the right. But Roethlisberger woefully underthrew the ball right to Herndon, who returned it a Super Bowl-record 76 yards to the 20.

"That was one where my mind was telling me to throw it over the top and my arm didn't throw it over the top," Roethlisberger said. "I read it right. I just didn't throw it good."

Three plays later, Seattle quarterback Matt Hasselbeck threw a 16-yard touchdown to tight end Jerramy Stevens, and the shocking turnaround left the Steelers holding a tenuous 14-10 lead instead of what might have been a 21-3 stranglehold.

It fell so quiet in Ford Field that you could hear the Seahawks fans.

Cowher Power

Matt Freed

It became deathly so a bit later when Stevens took an 18-yard pass to the Steelers' 1 that put Seattle on the brink of snatching a fourth-quarter lead. But the play was canceled by a holding penalty and, on the next snap, nose tackle Casey Hampton sacked Hasselbeck at the 34. On third down, Hasselbeck threw deep and poorly. Cornerback Ike Taylor, who dropped an early interception, picked this one off to preserve the Steelers' four-point lead.

It would spark another celebration four plays later.

On third-and-2 at Seattle's 43, Roethlisberger ran 5 yards on a draw from the shotgun. On the next play, he pitched to Parker and threw a block. Parker handed off to wide receiver Antwaan Randle El, who ran to the right, stopped and uncorked a perfect pass that Ward caught over cornerback Marcus Trufant at the 5 and ran into

the end zone for a 43-yard score.

It was the first touchdown pass by a wide receiver in the game's history, and it gave the Steelers a 21-10 lead with 8:56 left in the game.

"They called a great play at the right time," Ward said. "The offensive line did its job blocking, and El threw a hell of a ball."

The Steelers were fortunate to hold a 7-3 halftime lead. The Seahawks moved the ball offensively and smothered the Steelers on defense but had little to show for it, mainly because of untimely penalties.

"You can't make mistakes like that and expect to win against a good team like this," Hasselback said.

The Seahawks took a 3-0 lead with 22 seconds left

Bill Cowher is interviewed with his daughters at his side after the game.

in the first quarter on Josh Brown's 47-yard field goal, and the Steelers were lucky it wasn't worse They finally got something going after Ward ran 18 yards on a first down to their 48. But on the next play, Roethlisberger faked to Bettis and threw a deep ball that floated and was intercepted by safety Michael Boulware at the 17.

On the Steelers' next possession, Roethlisberger converted a third down by throwing 20 yards to Wilson. Ward dropped what would have been a 22-yard touchdown pass, and a 10-yard penalty and sack put the Steelers back to their 40, third-and 28.

Roethlisberger dropped back, scrambled away from a three-man rush and tiptoed up to the line of scrimmage. He stopped and heaved the ball deep toward the opposite side, to the right, the kind of play John Elway made famous. Ward out-muscled Boulware to make the catch at the 3.

Bettis got 2 yards on two carries and, on third down, Roethlisberger rolled left behind Bettis and plunged toward the goal line. The ball barely broke the plane of the goal line for a touchdown that was held up by a review.

It was the first time a Steelers quarterback scored in a Super Bowl.

The Steelers led, 7-3, and took that to halftime when Brown missed a 54-yard field goal wide with two seconds to go. Brown also would miss a 50-yarder in the second half.

"We're bringing the Super Bowl trophy back to Pittsburgh," linebacker Joey Porter said. "That's all that matters." ✦

Peter Diana

Jerome Bettis rumbled for 43 yards on 14 carries in his final game as a pro.

XL.

Mission Accomplished

Cowher finally gets the Steelers that "one for the thumb"

By Gene Collier, Post-Gazette Sports Writer

On the 15th day of his 15th year in the Steelers organization, Bill Cowher finally closed his fingers around the Vince Lombardi Trophy and presented it to Dan Rooney, the man who hired him Jan. 21, 1992, to pursue that very obelisk of Tiffany hardware.

This is the kind of spooky numerology that carries with it the unmistakable aura of predestination, but as Cowher stood ramrod straight in a dark suit behind one last downtown Detroit podium for some parting words on the import and the legacy of Super Bowl XL, he had no time for destiny delayed or destiny delivered, much less the destiny of timeline happenstance.

On the morning of what was merely the 16th day of his 15th year then, the guy with the best winning percentage in Steelers history resisted any calcification of his image or of his place in the game or the game's history.

"Are you defined by winning a Super Bowl?" he asked as the preamble to an answer. "I don't think that the destination defines you. It's the journey that defines you."

Ten hours before this, the journey had taken him to the only place he hadn't been, to the platform in the middle of a storm of confetti at the closing vortex of the Super Bowl, and though Sunday night's 21-10 victory against the Seattle Seawhawks did not appear to have altered his demeanor by even one molecule, it had left him exhilarated enough or just tired enough to reflect upon some things, among them: reflection.

"I am going to sit back and reflect," he said, almost seeming surprised those words could come out of his mouth in that order. "I always tell players never reflect, and I try to practice what I preach, but this next week, I'm going to do a whole lot of reflecting."

For a second there in the Renaissance Ballroom four stories above the Detroit River, I linked that statement to all the postgame talk about the beatitudes of going out on top, about how there's no better way for Jerome Bettis to walk away from this game than first, being able to walk, and second, by finishing with a Super Bowl victory.

"Why not Cowher?" came the silent question.

Right now this is a pretty decent little coaching career, is it not? It's produced a bunch of division titles and a roster of All-Pros and a couple of AFC championships, and now a Super Bowl victory and even talk of a square jawed Cowher bust in Canton one day. Will there be any better days than the 15th day of his 15th year?

"I'm going to do a lot of reflecting."

No. Ninety-nine chances in 100, Cowher will be back, but something definitely ended overnight

Lake Fong

Ben Roethlisberger shares a moment with Bill Cowher in the closing seconds of Super Bowl XL at Ford Field in Detroit.

Willie Parker scores in the third quarter of Super Bowl XL on a 75-yard run.

Matt Freed

Sunday. Cowher still may not believe you are defined by destinations in this game, but when you are for so long and with so much vitriol maligned for destinations unreached, a lot of things change when you finally get there.

And you could see the evidence in Cowher's candor yesterday. Some things he hadn't said and hadn't dreamed of saying publicly came out in his typically measured way, but came out nonetheless against his tradition of rhetorical minimalism.

"Those AFC championship losses are tough; they wear on you," he said of four home title games that dragged his postseason record to 8-9 as of last January. "When you go through those, it makes this all the more special. I told guys last week,

you've been through those losses, but when you lose the Super Bowl, it's twice as bad."

There is no calculating the psychological price to Cowher had his brilliant defense not arisen to bail out his jittery offense over the final three quarters at Ford Field the other night, but the man who now has won more postseason games than any active coach except Washington's Joe Gibbs let it be clear yesterday that he had a very high regard for this team even as it drew the sixth seed in the AFC playoffs, a post position from which no horse ever fled to the winner's circle.

Cowher Power

Lake Fong

Super Bowl XL MVP Hines Ward holds up the Vince Lombardi Trophy.

Bill Cowher exults in the middle of the craziness that was the Super Bowl XL victory celebration.

"We were a six seed," he said, "but we could have been a one seed."

Cowher never would have said that kind of thing without first getting his mitt on the Lombardi.

In fact, the main reason I went to the post Super Bowl news conference was just to see if Cowher would come out with the same material: "We haven't accomplished anything yet. All we've done is given ourselves an opportunity to focus on minicamp and the improvement we can make there just by taking it one day at a time and having everyone take responsibility for the best interests of our football team."

Or something.

But that's over now. You can say what you think a little more when you're a world champion. For now, Cowher's still not really sure what he thinks.

He'll reflect.

"The team of the '70s put Pittsburgh on the map," he said. "They created a tradition and legacy. We're proud of that tradition, and for us to say that we kind of did that, too, in 2005, well, it was neat to be a little part of that tradition this year." ✦

Lake Fong

Hines Ward and Jerome Bettis celebrate at the trophy presentation.

Super Bowl XL

SCORING BY QUARTERS

	1st	2nd	3rd	4th	Total
Seahawks	3	0	7	0	10
Steelers	0	7	7	7	21

SECOND QUARTER

Seattle: FG Brown 47, :22. Drive: 7 plays, 22 yards, 3:39. Key plays: Hasselbeck 20 pass to Jackson to Steelers 27; Hasselbeck 11 pass to Jurevicius. Seattle 3, Steelers 0.

SECOND QUARTER

Steelers: Roethlisberger 1 run (Reed kick), 1:55. Drive: 11 plays, 59 yards, 6:20. Key plays: Roethlisberger 12 pass to Ward on 3rd-and-6 to Seahawks 43; Roethlisberger 20 pass to Wilson; Roethlisberger 37 pass to Ward on 3rd-and-28 to Seahawks 3. Steelers 7, Seattle 3.

THIRD QUARTER

Steelers: Parker 75 run (Reed kick), 14:38. Drive: 2 plays, 75 yards, :22. Steelers 14, Seattle 3.

Seattle: Stevens 16 pass from Hasselbeck (Brown kick), 6:45. Drive: 3 plays, 20 yards, :53. Key play: Herndon 76 interception return to Steelers 20. Steelers 14, Seattle 10.

FOURTH QUARTER

Steelers: Ward 43 pass from Randle El (Reed kick), 8:56. Drive: 4 plays, 56 yards, 1:50. Key plays: Taylor 24 interception return to Steelers 29 plus Hasselbeck 15-yard low block penalty to Steelers 44; Roethlisberger 5 run on 3rd-and-

2. Steelers 21, Seattle 10 • Attendance: 68,206.

A CLOSER LOOK

SEATTLE		STEELERS	SEATTLE		STEELERS
20	FIRST DOWNS	14	26-49	Completed-Attempts	10-22
5	Rushing	6	1	Had Intercepted	2
15	Passing	8	5.0	Yards Per Pass Play	6.9
0	Penalty	0	3-2-1	KICKOFFS-END ZONE-TB	4-0-0
5-17	THIRD DOWN EFFICIENCY	8-15	6-50.2	PUNTS-AVERAGE	6-48.7
1-2	FOURTH DOWN EFFICIENCY	0-0	0	Punts blocked	0
396	TOTAL NET YARDS	339	0-0	FGs-PATs BLOCKED	0-0
77	Total Plays	56	174	TOTAL RETURN YARDAGE	99
5.1	Average Gain	6.1	4-27	Punt Returns	2-32
137	NET YARDS RUSHING	181	4-71	Kickoff Returns	2-43
25	Rushes	33	2-76	TOTAL Interceptions-Return Yards	1-24
5.5	Avgerage per rush	5.5	7-70	PENALTIES-YARDS	3-20
259	NET YARDS PASSING	158	0-0	FUMBLES-LOST	0-0
3-14	Sacked-Yards lost	1-8	33:02	TIME OF POSSESSION	26:58
273	Gross-Yards passing	166			

Cowher Power

RUSHING

SEATTLE

Alexander	20-95
Hasselbeck	3-35
Strong	2-7

STEELERS

Parker	10-93
Bettis	14-43
Roethlisberger	7-25
Ward	1-18
Haynes	1-2

PASSING

SEATTLE

Hasselbeck	26-49-1-273

STEELERS

Roethlisberger	9-21-2-123
Randle El	1-1-0-43

RECEIVING

SEATTLE

Engram	6-70
Jurevicius	5-93
Jackson	5-50
Stevens	3-25
Strong	2-15
Hannam	2-12
Alexander	2-2
Morris	1-6

STEELERS

Ward	5-123
Randle El	3-22
Wilson	1-20
Parker	1-1

PUNT RETURNS

SEATTLE

Warrick	4-27

STEELERS

Randle El	2-32

KICKOFF RETURNS

SEATTLE

Scobey	3-55
Morris	1-16

STEELERS

Colclough	2-43
Taylor	1-0

TACKLES - ASSISTS - SACKS

SEATTLE		STEELERS	
Hill	7-1-0	Taylor	6-1-0
Tatupu	6-3-0	Townsend	5-1-0
Pruitt	4-0-0	Haggans	5-0-0
Trufant	3-0-0	Farrior	4-2-0
Bernard	2-0-0	Foote	4-1-0
Boulware	2-3-0	Polamalu	4-1-0
Wistrom	2-0-1	Hampton	4-0-0
Lewis	2-2-0	Porter	3-0-0
Tubbs	2-0-0	A.Smith	3-1-0
Koutouvides	2-0-0	Keisel	2-0-0
Kacyvenski	1-0-0	Carter	2-1-0
Hasselbeck	1-0-0	Harrison	2-1-0
Darby	1-0-0	von Oelhoffen	2-0-0
Dyson	1-0-0	McFadden	2-0-0
Manuel	1-0-0	Hope	1-2-0
Herndon	0-1-0	Kriewaldt	1-1-0
		Iwuoma	1-0-0
		Colclough	1-0-0

INTERCEPTIONS

SEATTLE

Boulware	1-0
Herndon	1-76

STEELERS

None

MISSED FIELD GOALS

SEATTLE

Brown	54 (WR), 50 (WL)

STEELERS

None

OFFICIALS

Referee	Bill Leavy
Ump	Garth DeFelice
HL	Mark Hittner
LJ	Mark Perlman
FJ	Steve Zimmer
SJ	Tom Hill
BJ	Bob Waggoner
Replay	Bob Boyleston

Time: 3:36.

Hines Ward kisses the trophy
that will join the Steelers'
four others in Pittsburgh.

Lake Fong

Bill Cowher and his wife, Kaye, acknowledge the many fans who came out to salute the team during the victory parade in Pittsburgh.

Steve Mellon

Hines Ward, Jerome Bettis and Bill Cowher celebrate after winning Super Bowl XL.

Lake Fong

During their time together in Pittsburgh, Ben Roethlisberger and Bill Cowher have forged a relationship the entire city can smile about.

Peter Diana

Peter Diana

JEROME BETTIS

Running back • Height: 5-11 • Weights: 255 • Born: 02/16/1972 • College: Notre Dame

Year	G	Att	Yds	Avg	Lg	TD
1996	16	320	1431	4.5	50	11
1997	15	375	1665	4.4	34	7
1998	15	316	1185	3.8	42	3
1999	16	299	1091	3.6	35	7
2000	16	355	1341	3.8	30	8
2001	11	225	1072	4.8	48	4
2002	13	187	666	3.6	41	9
2003	16	246	811	3.3	21	7
2004	15	250	941	3.8	29	13
2005	12	110	368	3.3	39	9

Peter Diana

BEN ROETHLISBERGER

Quarterback • Height: 6-5 • Weight: 241 • Born: 03/02/1982 • College: Miami (Ohio)

Year	G	Att	Comp	Pct	Yds	TD	Int	Rate
2004	14	295	196	66.4	2621	17	11	98.1
2005	12	268	168	62.7	2385	17	9	98.6

Peter Diana

HINES WARD

Hines Ward • Wide receiver • Height: 6-0 • Weight: 215 • Born: 03/08/1976 • College: Georgia

Year	G	Rec	Yds	Avg	TD
1998	16	15	246	16.4	0
1999	16	61	638	10.5	7
2000	16	48	672	14.0	4
2001	16	94	1003	10.7	4
2002	16	112	1329	11.9	12
2003	16	95	1163	12.2	10
2004	16	80	1004	12.6	4
2005	15	69	975	14.1	11

Matt Freed

KORDELL STEWART

Quarterback • Height: 6-1 • Weight: 217 • Born: 10/16/1972 • College: Colorado

Year	G	Att	Cmp	Pct	Yds	TD	Int	Rate
1995	10	7	5	71.4	60	1	0	136.9
1996	16	30	11	36.7	100	0	2	18.8
1997	16	440	236	53.6	3020	21	17	75.2
1998	16	458	252	55.0	2560	11	18	62.9
1999	16	275	160	58.2	1464	6	10	64.9
2000	16	289	151	52.2	1860	11	8	73.6
2001	16	442	266	60.2	3109	14	11	81.7
2002	27	166	109	65.7	1155	6	6	82.8

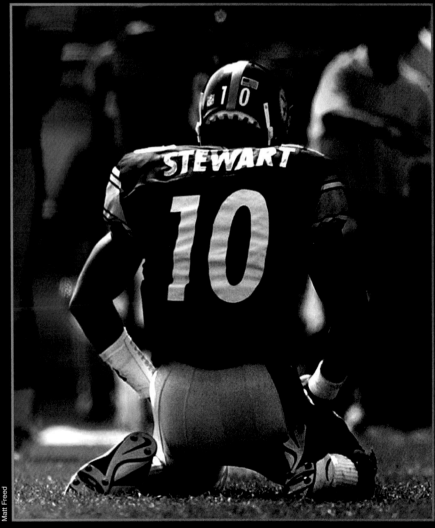

Matt Freed

Year	G	Tk	Ast	Sacks	Int	Yds	Avg	TD
2003	16	30	8	2	0	0	0	0
2004	16	67	29	1	5	58	11.6	1
2005	16	73	18	3	2	42	21.0	0

Matt Freed

Peter Diana

ROD WOODSON

Safety • Height: 6-0 • Weight: 205 • Born: 03/10/1965 • College: Purdue

Year	G	Tck	Ast	Sacks	Int	Yds	TD
1987	8	0	0	0	1	45	1
1988	16	0	0	0.5	4	98	0
1989	15	0	0	0	3	39	0
1990	16	0	0	0	5	67	0
1991	15	60	11	1	3	72	0
1992	16	70	12	6	4	90	0
1993	16	67	7	2	8	138	1
1994	15	65	15	3	4	109	2
1995	1	0	1	0	0	0	0
1996	16	61	10	1	6	121	1

Peter Diana